Richard Brothers

A Revealed Knowledge of the Prophecies and Times

Richard Brothers

A Revealed Knowledge of the Prophecies and Times

ISBN/EAN: 9783337248659

Printed in Europe, USA, Canada, Australia, Japan

Cover: Foto ©Lupo / pixelio.de

More available books at **www.hansebooks.com**

A REVEALED KNOWLEDGE

OF THE

Prophecies & Times

BOOK THE FIRST,

Wrote under the direction of the

LORD GOD,

And Published by his Sacred Command:

IT BEING THE

FIRST SIGN OF WARNING

FOR THE BENEFIT OF ALL NATIONS.

CONTAINING, WITH OTHER

GREAT AND REMARKABLE THINGS,

Not Revealed to any other Person on Earth,

THE

RESTORATION OF THE HEBREWS

TO JERUSALEM, BY THE YEAR OF 1798:

Under their Revealed

PRINCE AND PROPHET.

LONDON.

PRINTED IN THE YEAR OF CHRIST

1794.

PREFACE.

WHEN I was commanded to write the Chronology of the World, I was immediately after instructed by Revelation how; without which I could not, nor could any other Man on the face of the Earth with certainty, however eminent for Wisdom and Learning he might be: after it was done, the LORD GOD said to me in a vision at night,—That is the true Age of the World, and the general computed one is erroneous.

As the SCRIPTURE is the only great Fountain of Knowledge, or Book of written Truth in the World; as it contains the sacred Records of those Things which GOD has predetermined shall be hereafter—as well as those which have been already; and as it contains the History of our own Creation, with that of every living thing besides, It alone, in preference to any Man's opinion, ought to be, without the least doubt, freely believed and confidently depended on.

Although I am enabled, from revealed Knowledge, to write considerably more than what this Book contains, and which, in Justice to the Divine Spirit of Truth from whom it flows, ought to be believed; yet GOD, who instructs me in all things, that I may shew an Example of precision to the Learned, and be admired for it by the Wise; that I may give instruction to the Poor, and demonstrate the certainty of what I do write to every Man that has the least knowledge of his Creator, commands me to additionally Seal its Truth by that great Testimony of Scriptural Evidence which no Nation can deny, and which no human Arguments can oppose.

Therefore having Authority, I proceed through the Scripture, regularly uncovering, by revealed Knowledge as I go, its sacred Records WHICH HAVE BEEN PRESERVED FOR ME, holding each one up for public View, beautiful and clear to the open mind; that all Men may behold and examine them, that all men may perceive their Truth, and admire at this late Hour of the World, not only what was wrote by Daniel at Babylon, EXPLAINED IN LONDON, but likewise a similar Communication of REVEALED KNOWLEDGE.

IN obedience to the Sacred Command of the Lord God, whose Servant and Prophet I am, I publish this writing, that it may be translated into all Languages, for the information and benefit of all Nations.

THE TRUE AGE OF THE WORLD.

	Years.		Years
Adam was	130	Old when Seth was born.—Lived in all	930
Seth -	105	- - - - - - - - - - -	912
Enos -	90	- - - - - - - - - - -	905
Cainan -	70	- - - - - - - - - - -	910
Mahalaleel	65	- - - - - - - - - - -	895
Jared -	162	- - - - - - - - - - -	962
Enoch -	65	- - - - - - - - - - -	365
Methuselah	187	- - - - - - - - - - -	969
Lamech -	182	- - - - - - - - - - -	777
Noah	500	- - - - - - - - - - -	950
Shem was	born	Old at the Flood.	

1656 *From the Creation to the Flood.*

The genealogy is reckoned to and from Shem; two years after the Flood, Arphaxad was born to him.

Shem -	02	Lived after the birth of his Son	500
Arphaxed -	35	- - - - - - - -	403
Salah -	30	- - - - - - - -	403
Eber -	34	- - - - - - - -	430
Peleg -	30	- - - - - - - -	209
Reu -	32	- - - - - - - -	207
Serug -	30	- - - - - - - -	200
Nahor -	29	- - - - - - - -	119
Terah -	70	- - - - Lived in all	205

292 *From the Flood to the birth of Abraham.*

Abraham was	100	Old when Isaac was born—Lived in all	175
Isaac -	60	- - - - - - - -	180
Jacob -	130	Toll living in Egypt with his children.	147

290

430 The children of Israel lived in Egypt.
480 From the children of Israel leaving Egypt to the foundation of the Temple.

A 2

In the 4th year and *2d month of Solomon's Reign the foundation of the Temple was laid.

	Years.		Years.
Solomon *reigned* 36 after the Temple begun building: in all			40
Rehoboam *in all* 17		Begun to reign at the age of	41
Abijam	3		
Asa	41		
Jehoshaphat	25		35
Jehoram	8		32
Ahaziah	1		22
Queen Athaliah	6		
Jehoash	40		7
Amaziah	29		25
Azariah	52		16
Jotham	16		25
Ahaz	16		20
Hezekiah	29		25
Manasseh	55		12
Amon	2		22
Josiah	31		8
Jehoahaz	0	3 Months	23
Jehoiakim	11	0	25
Jehoiachin	0	8	18

418 6 The beginning of the Recorded Captivity, in the
             eighth year of Nebuchadnezzar's reign.
Zedekiah †11 8* From the foundation of the Temple to its
                    destruction.

Nebuchadn. *reign'd* 39 After the Recorded Captivity began: in all
Evil Merodach 11   over Babylon 45
Belshazzar   22

70 The Jewish Captivity at Babylon: that the
     word of the Lord to Jeremiah the prophet might be fulfilled, which was,—
     And all nations shall serve him, his son,
     and his son's son.—Chap. xxvii. 7.

69 Weeks, or 483 Years, from the command of Cyrus to restore
             the Jews to the birth of Christ, the Messiah
             and King.

4119 The age of the World when Christ was born.
1794

5913 The age of the World, this present year of
                                                    1794

† Not included in the Chronology.

THE first knowledge of that LAW, which was committed to writing by MOSES, was given to Abraham at the age of 99, or of the world 2047.

The GOSPEL OF SALVATION was first preached by CHRIST, at the age of 30—of the World 4149.

JERUSALEM was besieged and taken three different times by Nebuchadnezzar.—The first was in the reign of Jehoiakim, when several of the Princes and Priests were carried away to Babylon; among the former was Daniel, and among the latter was Ezekiel:—both prophets. The second was in the reign of Jehoiachim, *when the Recorded Captivity began:* and the third was in the reign of Zedekiah, when the TEMPLE and CITY were levelled with the ground.

OF THE

MESSIAH.

The Prophet DANIEL, CHAP. IX.

Verse 25. Know therefore and understand, that from the going forth of the command to restore *(meaning the Captivity)* and to build Jerusalem to MESSIAH THE PRINCE, shall be seven weeks, and three-score and two weeks; the street shall be built again, and the wall even in troublesome times.

Seven weeks and three-score and two weeks, is meant for a time of *four hundred and eighty-three years:* which commenced in the first year of Cyrus over Babylon, when he issued the Proclamation to restore the Captivity, and concluded at the birth of Christ.

Two years after the Jews returned from Babylon to Jerusalem they laid the foundation of the second temple, but were so much interrupted in the building as not to be able to complete it until the expiration of eighty-two years.

26. And after Three-score and two weeks (which is *Four hundred and Thirty-four years,* meaning from the time the Temple was finished to the death of Christ) shall Messiah be cut off, but not for himself; and the People of the Prince that comes, *(meaning the Romans)* will destroy the City and the Sanctuary; it will be done, like the overflowing of a flood: and to the end of war, their desolation is determined.

While war continues in the world, JERUSALEM, the Capital of the KING OF PEACE is decreed to lie desolate: the restoration of the Jews will commence with the destruction of war, to favour their return and build the City; when all nations will rejoice with them and once more receive from Jerusalem the commands of the living God.

The

[6]

The Prophet ISAIAH, CHAP. VII.

14. Therefore the Lord himself will give you a sign : behold, a Virgin shall conceive and bear a SON, and shall call his name IMMANUEL.

This was the LORD JESUS CHRIST, who was born of the BLESSED VIRGIN called MARY.

CHAP. IX. 6 v. For unto us *a child is born,* unto us *a son is given;* and the government shall be on his shoulder: and his name shall be called WONDERFUL COUNSELLOR, THE MIGHTY GOD, THE EVERLASTING FATHER, THE PRINCE OF PEACE.

This was the LORD JESUS CHRIST, who was the MESSIAH AND KING OF THE JEWS.—

7. Of the increase of his Government and peace there shall be no end, upon the Throne of David, and upon his Kingdom, to order it, and to establish it with judgement and with justice, from henceforth even for ever: the zeal of the Lord of Hosts will perform this.

The Prophet ZACHARIAH, CHAP. XII.

10. And I will pour upon the house of David, and upon the Inhabitants of Jerusalem, the spirit of grace and of supplications: and they shall look to me that was pierced; and shall mourn, like him that mourns for his only son; and shall be in bitterness, like him that is in bitterness for his first born.

This verse will be fulfilled by the Jews after their Return, it means the Lord Jesus Christ who was crucified at the age of *Thirty-three years and four months.*—Told me by Revelation.

THE DEPARTURE OF THE HEBREWS FROM ALL NATIONS, AND THEIR RETURN TO JERUSALEM.

From the *Three thousand Six hundred and Seventeenth year of the World,* which was the third year of Belshazzar King of Babylon, when the Vision was shewn to Daniel, of Jerusalem's future desolation, the last dispersion of the Jews, and their being trod under foot in all Nations,—to the time of their Return in the latter days;—is TWO THOUSAND THREE HUNDRED YEARS.

To make the vision of Daniel, which was explained to me by Revelation from the Lord God, to be more easily understood,— Read what follows.

The Prophet Daniel, after describing the succession of Cyrus and Alexander, goes on to the time of Christ, the destruction of Jerusalem, and how long it is to lie desolate; the dispersion of the Jews, and how long they are to be trod under foot in all Nations.

CHAP.

CHAP. VIII. 11. v. Yea, he magnified himself, even to the PRINCE OF THE HOST; by him the DAILY SACRIFICE was taken away, and the PLACE of his sanctuary was cast down.

12. And a Host was given him against the daily sacrifice by reason of transgression: and it cast down the TRUTH to the ground, and it practised and prospered.

13. Then I heard one Saint speaking, and another Saint said to that certain saint which spake, How long shall be the Vision concerning the Daily sacrifice, and the transgression of delolation, to give both the SANCTUARY and the HOST to be trodden under foot?

One ANGEL was asking another in the presence of Daniel, that he might hear and be informed to write down what was said.

The Sanctuary meant the second temple, though not built when this Vision was shewn to Daniel; the Host, the multitude of the people, or the whole nation.

How long shall be the Vision, means, how long is it from this time or year of shewing the Vision to Daniel until it is fulfilled by the restoration of the Jews, in the latter days of the World, when the CURSE for *transgression* which made the city desolate will be removed, and the ground of the Sanctuary cleaned.

14. And he said to me, unto *Two thousand and three hundred days*; then shall the Sanctuary be cleaned.

Days are mentioned by the angel instead of years, to conceal the meaning of the prophecy until the proper time is fulfilled and the appointed person made known for it to be revealed to: the present is the time that was then intended; I am the appointed person for it to be revealed to, and the Prophet commanded to make it known.

3617—The year of the World when the Vision was shewn to Daniel of Jerusalem's future desolation, and how long.

2300—From the year of shewing the Vision to the restoration of the Jews, when it will be fulfilled.

5917—The year of the world when the Jews will be restored to Jerusalem, which answers to the year of Christ 1798.

The return of the JEWS to their own Land in the latter time of the World, recorded by Moses, and the other Prophets.

This Song of Moses, in the Thirty-second chapter of Deuteronomy, is the written testimony given then, between God as Christ, and his people, until their return to Jerusalem in the latter days of the World. It begins with describing Christ preaching the Gospel of the Kingdom of Heaven, afterwards the great destruction of the Jews, which was fulfilled by the Romans, and their dispersion over the world: the latter part means their restoration, which invites all nations to rejoice with them for the abundant mercy of God, and his goodness to their Land.

DEUTERONOMY, CHAP. XXXII.

1 v. Give ear, O ye Heavens, and I will speak, and hear, O earth, the words of my mouth.

2. My doctrine shall drop as the rain: my speech shall distil as the dew, as the small rain upon the tender herb, and as the showers upon the grafs.

3. Because I will publish the name of the Lord: ascribe ye greatnefs to our God.

4. He is the ROCK, his work is perfect; for all his ways are judgement: a God of truth, and without iniquity, juft and right is he.

Compare this part to the preaching of Chrift in the beginning of the fifth chapter of the Gofpel by St. Matthew, and fee how nearly they agree.

21. They have moved me to Jealoufy with that which is not God; they have provoked me to anger with their vanities; and I will move them to Jealoufy with thofe which are not a people, I will provoke them to anger with a foolifh nation.

22. For a fire is kindled in mine anger, and fhall burn to the lowest hell, and fhall confume the earth with her increase, and fet on fire the foundations of the mountains.

23. I will heap mifchiefs upon them, I will fpend my arrows upon them.

24. They fhall be burnt with hunger, and devoured with burning heat, and with bitter deftruction: I will alfo fend the teeth of beafts upon them, with the poifon of ferpents of the duft.

25. The fword without, and terror within, fhall deftroy both the young man and the virgin, and the fuckling alfo with the man of grey hairs.

26. I faid, I would fcatter them into corners, I would make the remembrance of them to ceafe from among men.

27. Were it not that I feared the wrath of the enemy, left their adverfaries fhould behave themfelves ftrangely, and left they fhould fay, Our hand is high, and the Lord hath not done all this.

28. For they are a nation void of counfel, neither is there any underftanding in them.

Had God in his great anger deftroyed the Jews entirely by the Romans, they would have afcribed it to their own power, and after nations would not believe there ever had been fuch a people on the face of the earth: for which he difperfed them over the world to be travelling figns of warning to all nations until the determined time of their punifhment is expired, when he will, to fulfil the Scripture, recall them with mercy and everlasting love.

29. O that they were wife, that they underftood all'this, that they would confider their latter end.

30. How fhould one chafe a thoufand, and two put ten thoufand to flight, except their Rock had fold them, and the Lord had fhut them up?

36. For the Lord will judge his people, and repent himfelf for his fervants, when he fees that their power is gone, and there is none fhut up, or left.

37. And he fhall fay, where are their gods, their rock in whom they trufted;

38. Which did eat the fat of their facrifices, and drank the wine of their drink offerings? Let them rife up and help you, and be your protection.

39. See now that I, even I am he, (meaning God as Chrift, the Meffiah) and there is no God with me; I kill, and I make alive; I wound, and I heal; neither is there any that can deliver out of my hand.

40. For I lift up my hand to Heaven, and fay, I live for ever.

41. If I whet my glittering fword, and my hand take hold on judgement; I will render vengeance to my enemies, and will reward them that hate me.

42. I will make my arrows drunk with blood, and my fword fhall devour flefh; and that with the blood of the flain and of the captives, from the beginning of revenges upon the enemy.

43. REJOICE, O ye Nations, with his People, for he will avenge the blood of his fervants, and will render vengeance to his adverfaries, and will be merciful to his land, and to his people.

The Prophet ISAIAH, CHAP. II.

2. And it fhall come to pafs IN THE LAST DAYS that the mountain of the Lord's Houfe fhall be eftablifhed in the top of the mountains, and fhall be exalted above the hills, and all nations fhall flow to it.

3. And many people fhall go and fay Come ye, and let us go up to the mountain of the Lord, to the Houfe of the God of Jacob: and he will teach us his ways, and we will walk in his paths: for out of Zion fhall go forth the law, and the word of the Lord from Jerufalem.

And He (*This Prophecy, as every man of underftanding in the Scripture muft acknowledge, has never been fulfilled yet; for the time alluded to by the* Prophet, *is, according to his own words in the 2nd and 4th verfes, in the latter days of the world:* it is a Man that is alluded to, compofed of flefh and blood, of the tribe of Judah, of the family of David, *and not the Lord Jefus Chrift as all European nations fuppofe,* that is to fulfil this very exalted character:—going forth by Command and under the mighty

B power

power of GOD, *as his Elijah,* the laſt Prophet and Meſſenger, to warn all nations,—to turn the Fathers to the Children and the Children to their Fathers;—*to prepare them by univerſal Peace to receive a ſecond time* CHRIST *their* GOD *and* CREATOR) ſhall judge among the nations, and ſhall rebuke many people; and they ſhall beat their ſwords into plowſhares and their ſpears into reaping hooks; nation ſhall not lift up ſword againſt nation, neither ſhall they learn war any more.

All the nations of Europe acknowledge Chriſt for the Prince of Peace, and that his doctrine prohibits war; yet to the ſhame of all nations, they refuſe to obey his commands,—For which, as he beſeeched before and no nation would obey, he will ſoon command, when all nations muſt obey or be burnt with fire.

Chap. xi. 1 v. And there ſhall come forth a ROD out of the Stem of JESSE, and a BRANCH (meaning myſelf) ſhall grow out of his Roots:

2. And the SPIRIT of the LORD ſhall reſt upon him; the Spirit of Wiſdom and Underſtanding, the Spirit of Counſel and Might; the Spirit of knowledge, and of the fear of the Lord:

3. And ſhall make him of quick underſtanding in the fear of the Lord. And he ſhall not Judge after the ſight of his eyes, neither reprove after the hearing of his Ears:

4. But with righteouſneſs he will judge the POOR, *and Reprove with Equity for the* MEEK *of the earth:* and he ſhall ſmite the earth with the rod of his mouth, and with the breath of his lips he ſhall ſlay the wicked.

5. And righteouſneſs ſhall be the girdle of his loins, and faithfulneſs the girdle of his reins.

6. The Wolf alſo ſhall dwell with the Lamb, and the Leopard ſhall lie down with the Kid; and the Calf, and the young Lion, and the Fatling together; and a little Child ſhall lead them.

7. And the Cow, and the Bear ſhall feed; their young ones ſhall lie down together: and the Lion ſhall eat ſtraw like the Ox.

8. And the *Sucking Child* ſhall play on the hole of the Aſp, and the *Weaned Child* ſhall put his hand on the Cockatrice den.

9. They ſhall not deſtroy *nor hurt* in all my holy mountain: for the earth ſhall be full of the knowledge of the Lord, as the waters cover the ſea.

10. And in that day there ſhall be a ROOT OF JESSE, (meaning myſelf) which ſhall ſtand for a SIGN to the People (meaning the Jews,) to it ſhall the gentiles ſeek; and his REST, (meaning his government at Jeruſalem) ſhall be glorious.

When I was writing the firſt edition of this book for public information, I ſaid to God, *almoſt ſimilar to what the Prophet Samuel ſaid when he was commanded to anoint David to be king of Iſrael during the life time of Saul, for indeed I was fearful of being uſed ill,* I ſhall be called a falſe Prophet, and every body will ſay I am arrogating to myſelf the place of Chriſt: for the Engliſh and other European nations profeſſing chriſtianity, have always ſuppoſed that the ROD out of the STEM OF JESSE

alluded

alluded to in this chapter meant the LORD JESUS CHRIST: indeed it does not, but a man compofed of *flefh and blood* like one of themfelves, who is to be the greateft under heaven, and more power given to him from GOD than ever was—or ever will be to any other.

Like KING DAVID he will be empowered to command, and like the PROPHET ELIJAH he will be empowered to execute.

The LORD GOD commands me now to mention thefe things, to acknowledge the error (*though permitted to remove my unjuft apprehenfions for the confequences*) and with fhame my own criminality for doubting when he told me, and when I knew from his many records in the fcripture and from his many revealed promifes to myfelf—that he was bound by the facred truth of his WORDS to fulfil his covenant and protect me.

This writing I fign and date by command of the Lord God,— to remove my feeble error, and fubftitute without difguife (*for the falfe opinions of men are to be changed*) his all juft and powerful truth.

RICHARD BROTHERS.

LONDON, 10th of the Month called JULY, 1794.

11. And it fhall come to pafs in that day that the Lord will fet his hand again the fecond time to recover the remnant of his people, which are left, from Affyria, and from Egypt, and from Pathros, and from Cush, and from Elam, and from Shinar, and from Hamath, and from the iflands of the fea.

12. And he will fet up an enfign for the nations, and will affemble the outcafts of Ifrael, and gather together the difperfed of Judah from the four corners of the earth.

The firft captivity of the Jews was by Nebuchadnezzar, and their fecond by the Romans; their refidence in Egypt not being the confequence of conqueft, is not accounted as a captivity, becaufe they willingly entered into that country to be relieved from the diftreffes of famine in their own. The hard bondage they were oppreffed with proceeded from the Egyptians growing jealous of their quick multiplication and great numbers: but that did not take place until the death of Jofeph, and until fuch a confiderable time after had elapfed, as to wear away all remembrance of his name and gratitude for his kindnefs.

13. The envy alfo of Ephraim fhall depart, and the adverfaries of Judah fhall be cut off; Ephraim fhall not envy Judah, and Judah fhall not vex Ephraim.

14. But they fhall fly upon the fhoulders of the Philiftines towards the weft; they fhall fpoil them of the eaft together: they fhall lay their hand upon Moab and Edom; and the children of Ammon fhall obey them.

15. And the Lord will utterly deftroy the *tongue of the Egyptian fea*; and with his mighty wind he will fhake his hand over the river.

[12]

river, and smite it in the seven streams that men may go over dry shod.

16. And there shall be a highway from Assyria for the remnant of his people which are left ; like as it was to Israel in the day that he came up from the land of Egypt.

Chap. xii. And in that Day thou shalt say, O Lord I will praise thee : though thou was angry with me, thy anger is turned away, and thou comfortest me. Behold God is my salvation ; I will trust, and not be afraid for the LORD JEHOVAH is my strength and my song ; he also is become my salvation.

Therefore with joy he shall draw water out of the wells of salvation.

And in that day ye shall say, Praise the Lord, call upon his name, declare his doings among the people, and make mention that his name be exalted. Sing unto the Lord, for he has done excellent things ; this is known in all the earth. Cry out and shout, thou inhabitant of Zion : for great is the Holy one of Israel in the midst of thee.

Chap. liv. 1 v. SING, O BARREN, thou that didst not bear : break forth into singing, and cry aloud, thou that didst not travail with child ; for more are the children of the desolate, than the children of the married wife, says the Lord.

The married wife means Jerusalem at a former time, when rich and full of inhabitants ; the desolate wife means Jerusalem at present : although she is a heap of rubbish and levelled with the ground, the Jews will return in such great multitudes, that when rebuilt, her extent and number of people will be far greater than at any former period.

This is the true meaning of the prophecy, and not the Gentiles deliverance, as is placed at the head of the chapter in the Bible.

2. Enlarge the place of thy tent, and let them stretch forth the curtains of thy habitation : spare not, lengthen thy cords, and strengthen thy stakes.

3. For thou shalt break forth on the right hand, and on the left ; and thy seed shall inherit the Gentiles, and make the desolate cities to be inhabited.

4. Fear not, for thou shalt not be ashamed : neither be thou confounded : for thou shalt not be put to shame ; for thou shalt forget the shame of thy youth, and shall not remember the reproach of thy widowhood any more.

5. For thy Maker is thy husband ; the Lord of Hosts is his name : and thy Redeemer the Holy one of Israel, the God of the whole earth shall he be called.

6. For the Lord has called thee as a woman forsaken and grieved in spirit, and a wife of youth, when thou wast refused.

7. For a small moment I have forsaken thee, but with great mercies I will gather thee.

8. In

8. In a little wrath I hid my face from thee, for a moment; but with everlasting kindness I will have mercy on thee, says the Lord my Redeemer.

9. For this is as the waters of Noah to me: for as I have sworn that the waters of Noah should not go over the earth any more, so have I sworn that I would not be wrath with thee, nor rebuke thee.

10. For the mountains shall depart, and the hills be removed: but my kindness shall not depart from thee, neither shall the covenant of my peace be removed, says the Lord, that has mercy on thee.

Chap. LX. 1. ARISE, shine: for thy light is come, and the glory of the Lord is risen upon thee.

2. For, behold, the darkness shall cover the earth, and gross darkness the people; but the Lord will rise upon thee, and his glory will be seen upon thee.

3. And the Gentiles shall come to thy light, and Kings to the brightness of thy rising.

8. Who are these that come as a Cloud, and that fly as the Doves to their windows?

9. Surely the Isles shall wait on me; but the ships of Tarshish first, to bring thy sons from afar, their gold and silver with them, to the name of the Lord thy God, and to the Holy One of Israel, because he has glorified thee.

10. And the sons of strangers shall build up thy walls, and their kings shall minister to thee; for in my wrath I smote thee, but in my favour I will have mercy on thee.

11. Therefore thy gates shall be open continually; they shall not be shut day or night: that men may bring to thee the forces of the Gentiles, and that their kings may be brought.

12. For the nation and kingdom that will not serve thee shall perish; yea, those nations shall be utterly wasted.

13. The glory of Lebanon shall come to thee, the Fir-tree, the Pine-tree, and the Box together, to beautify the place of my Sanctuary: for I will make the place of MY FEET glorious.

14. The sons also of them that afflicted thee shall come bending to thee, and all they that despised thee shall bow themselves down to the soles of thy feet; and they shall call thee—THE CITY OF THE LORD, the Zion of the Holy One of Israel.

15. Whereas thou hast been forsaken and hated, so that no man went through thee; I will make thee an eternal excellency, a joy of many generations.

16. Thou shalt also suck the milk of the Gentiles, and shalt suck the breasts of kings: and thou shalt know that I the Lord am thy Saviour and thy Redeemer, the mighty One of Jacob.

17. For brass I will bring gold, and for iron I will bring silver; for wood brass, and for stones iron: I will also make thy officers Peace, and thy exactors Righteousness.

18. Vio-

18. Violence shall no more be heard in thy land, wasting nor destruction within thy borders; but thou shalt call thy walls Salvation, and thy gates praise.

19. The Sun shall be no more thy Light by Day, neither for brightness the Moon by Night; but the Lord will be to thee an everlasting light, and thy God thy glory.

20. Thy Sun shall no more go down, neither shall thy moon withdraw itself: for the Lord will be thy everlasting light, and the days of thy mourning shall be ended.

21. Thy people also shall be all righteous, they shall inherit the land for ever; the branch of my planting, and the work of my hands, that I may be glorified.

22. A little one shall become a thousand, and a great one a strong nation. I the Lord will hasten it in due time.

Chap. LXII. For Zion's sake I will not hold my peace, and for Jerusalem's sake I will not rest, until the righteousness thereof go forth as brightness, and the salvation thereof as a lamp that burns.

4. Thou shalt no more be termed forsaken, neither shall thy land any more be termed desolate; but thou shalt be called HEPHZIBAH, and thy land BEULAH. For the Lord delights in thee, AND THY LAND SHALL BE MARRIED.

8. The Lord has sworn by his Right hand, and by the Arm of his strength; surely I will no more give thy corn to be meat for thy enemies, and the sons of the stranger shall no more drink the wine for which thou hast laboured.

9. But they that gather it shall eat it, and praise the Lord; and they that bring it together, shall drink it in the courts of my holiness.

10. Go through, go through the gates; prepare ye the way of the people; cast up, cast up the highway; gather out the stones; lift up a standard for the people.

11. Behold, the Lord has proclaimed to the end of the world, say ye to the daughter of Zion, behold thy salvation comes; behold his reward is with him, and his work before him.

12. And they shall call them, THE HOLY PEOPLE, the Redeemed of the Lord; and thou shalt be called Sought Out, A CITY NOT FORSAKEN.

Chap. LXV. 17. For, behold, I create new Heavens and a new Earth! and the former shall not be remembered, nor come into mind.

18. But be ye glad, and rejoice for ever in that which I create; for, behold, I create Jerusalem a rejoicing, and her people a joy.

19. And I will rejoice in Jerusalem, and be joyful in my people: the voice of weeping shall be no more heard in her, nor the voice of crying.

23. They

23. They shall not labour in vain, nor bring forth for nothing; for they are the seed which the Lord has blessed, and their offspring with them.

24. And it shall come to pass, that before they call I will answer; and while they are yet speaking, I will hear.

25. The Wolf and the Lamb shall feed together, and the Lion shall eat straw like the Bullock; and dust shall be the serpent's meat. They shall not destroy, nor hurt, in all my holy mountain, says the Lord.

This last verse is an allusion to the peace and great happiness that will be in the land of Israel when the Jews are restored.

Chap. LXVI. 10. Rejoice ye with Jerusalem, and be glad all ye that love her; rejoice with joy all ye that have mourned for her.

11. That ye may suck and be satisfied from the breasts of her consolations; that ye may milk out and be delighted with the abundance of her glory.

12. For thus says the Lord; Behold I will extend peace to her like a river, and the glory of the Gentiles like a flowing stream; then ye shall suck—ye shall be borne upon her sides, and dandled upon her knees.

13. As one whom his mother comforts, so will I comfort you; and ye shall be comforted in Jerusalem.

14. And when ye see this, your heart shall rejoice and your bones shall flourish like an herb; and the hand of the Lord shall be known toward his servants, but his indignation toward his enemies.

15. For, behold, the Lord will come with fire, and with his chariots like a whirlwind; to render his anger with fury, and his rebuke with a flame of fire.

16. For by his fire, and by his sword, will the Lord plead with all flesh; and the slain of the Lord will be many.

20. And they shall bring all your Brethren for an offering to the Lord out of all nations, upon Horses, and in Chariots; upon Mules, and upon Swift Beasts, to my holy mountain Jerusalem, says the Lord; as the children of Israel bring an offering in a clean vessel into the House of the Lord.

21. And I will also take of them for Priests and for Levites, says the Lord.

22. For as the new Heavens and the new Earth which I will make, shall remain before me, says the Lord, so shall your seed and your name remain.

23. And it shall come to pass, that from one new Moon to another, and from one Sabbath to another, all people shall come to worship before me, says the Lord.

24. And they shall go forth and look upon the carcases of the men that have transgressed against me; for their worm shall not die, neither shall their fire be quenched, that they may be an abhorrence to all flesh.

The

The new Heavens and the new Earth, mean an entire regeneration of man through the power and knowledge from the Spirit of God. At present, all nations oppose the GOSPEL OF THE KINGDOM OF HEAVEN in the two most essential commands for them to obey, which are, War—and Swearing. Remember that form of praying, called the Lord's Prayer; which says, *Thy will be done on Earth, as it is in Heaven*. There is no war in Heaven, neither is there any Swearing: how is it then that the people of Europe, the most numerous professing Christianity, and certainly the most enlightened with knowledge of any in the world, can seriously say to God, Thy will be done on Earth, when they are instructed by their public laws and forms of worship to oppose it?

Although national laws are undesignedly made to oppose Christ, it is a duty incumbent on the people to take care that none of their prayers are: but that every supplication, and all their forms of worship are, as they should be—in strict obedience to his blessed Gospel of Peace.

The Prophet JEREMIAH, Chap. XXIII.

3. And I will gather the remnant of my flock out of all countries whither I have driven them, and will bring them again to their folds; and they shall be fruitful and increase.

4. And I will set shepherds over them which shall feed them: and they shall fear no more, nor be dismayed; neither shall they be lacking, says the Lord.

5. Behold the days are coming, says the Lord, that I will raise to David a righteous branch, and a king shall reign and prosper, and shall execute judgment and justice in the earth.

6. In his days Judah shall be saved, and Israel shall dwell safely; and this is the name wherewith he shall be called, The Lord's Righteousness. (*but not the Lord our Righteousness.*)

7. Therefore, behold the days are coming, says the Lord, when they shall no more say, the Lord lives that brought up the children of Israel out of the land of Egypt.

8. But the Lord lives who brought up and who led the seed of the house of Israel out of the North Country, and from all countries whither I had driven them; and they shall dwell in their own land.

Chap. XXXI. 1. At the same time, says the Lord, I will be the God of all the families of Israel, and they shall be my people.

2. Thus says the Lord, The people which were left from the sword found grace in the wilderness, even Israel when I went to cause him to rest.

3. The Lord has appeared to me of old, saying, Yes, I have loved thee with an everlasting love; therefore with loving-kindness I have drawn thee.

4. Again I will build thee, and thou shalt be built, O VIRGIN, OF ISRAEL; thou shalt again be adorned with thy tabrets, and shall go forth in the dances like them that make merry.

5. Thou

5. Thou shalt yet plant Vines on the mountains of Samaria; the planters shall plant, and thou shalt eat them as common things.

6. For there shall be a day when the watchmen on Mount Ephraim shall cry, Arise ye, and let us go up to Zion to the Lord our God.

7. For thus says the Lord; Sing with gladness for Jacob, and shout among the chief of the nations: publish, praise ye, and say, O Lord, save thy people, the remnant of Israel.

8. BEHOLD, I will bring them from the North country, and gather them from the Coasts of the Earth: the blind and the lame, the woman with child, and her that travails with child together: a great company shall return hither.

9. They shall come with weeping, and with supplications I will lead them: I will cause them to walk by the rivers of waters, in a straight way where they shall not stumble: for I am a father to Israel, and Ephraim is my first born.

10. Hear the word of the Lord, O ye nations, and declare it to the islands afar off; and say, he that scattered Israel will gather him, and keep him as a shepherd does his flock.

11. For the LORD has redeemed Jacob, and ransomed him from the Hand that was stronger than he.

12. Therefore they shall come and sing in the height of Zion, and shall flow together to the goodness of the Lord; for wheat, and for wine, and for oil, and for the young of the flock, and of the herd: and their soul shall be as a watered garden, *and they shall not sorrow any more at all.*

13. Then shall the Virgin rejoice in the dance, with young men and old together; for I will turn their mourning into joy, and will comfort them, and make them rejoice from their sorrow.

14. And I will satiate the soul of the priests with fatness, and my people shall be satisfied with my goodness, says the Lord.

15. Thus says the Lord; A voice was heard in Ramah, lamentation and bitter weeping; Rachael weeping for her children, refused to be comforted because they are not.

16. Thus says the Lord; Refrain thy voice from weeping, and thy eyes from tears: for thy work shall be rewarded, says the Lord; and they shall come again from the land of the enemy.

17. And there is hope in thy end, says the Lord, that thy children shall come again to their own border.

21. Set thee up waymarks, make thee high heaps: set thy heart toward the highway, even the way which thou went: turn again, O Virgin of Israel, turn again to these thy Cities.

22. How long wilt thou go about, O thou backsliding daughter? For the Lord has created a new thing in the Earth, A woman shall compass a man, (*It means Christ being born of the blessed Virgin.*)

23. Thus says the Lord of Hosts, the God of Israel; as yet they shall use this speech in the land of Judah, and in the cities thereof, when I bring again their captivity; THE LORD BLESS

BLESS THEE, O HABITATION OF JUSTICE, and Mountain of Holiness.

24. And there shall dwell in Judah itself, and in all the cities thereof together, husbandmen, and they that go forth with flocks.

25. For I will refresh the weary soul, and I will comfort every sorrowful soul.

31. Behold the days are coming, says the Lord, when I will make A NEW COVENANT with the House of Israel, and with the House of Judah.

32. Not according to the covenant I made with their fathers in the day that I took them by the hand to bring them out of the land of Egypt; which covenant they broke, although I was a husband to them, says the Lord.

33. But this shall be the covenant that I will make with the house of Israel; after those days, says the Lord, I will put my law in their inward parts, and write it in their hearts; and I will be their God, and they shall be my people.

34. And they shall teach no more every man his neighbour, and every man his brother, saying, Know the Lord: for they all shall know me, from the least of them to the greatest, says the Lord: for I will forgive their iniquity; and their sin I'll remember no more.

35. Thus says the Lord; who gives the sun for a light by day; and the ordinances of the stars for a light by night; who divides the sea when the waves of it roar: the Lord of Hosts is his name.

36. If those Ordinances depart from before me, says the Lord, then the SEED OF ISRAEL, shall also cease from being a Nation before me for ever.

37. Thus says the Lord; If Heaven above can be measured, and the foundations of the earth searched out beneath, I will also cast off the seed of Israel for all that they have done, says the Lord.

38. Behold the days are coming, says the Lord, when the City shall be built to the Lord from the Tower of Hananeel to the Gate of the corner.

39. And the measuring line shall yet go forth over against it on the hill Gareb, and shall compass about to Goath.

40. And the whole valley of the dead bodies and of the ashes, and all the fields to the brook of Kidron, to the corner of the horse gate toward the East, shall be Holy to the Lord: *it shall not be plucked up, nor thrown down any more for ever.*

The Prophet EZEKIEL, CHAP. XVI.

59. For thus says the Lord God: I will even deal with thee as thou hast done, which has despised the Oath by breaking the Covenant.

60. Nevertheless I will remember my Covenant with thee in the days of thy youth, but I will establish to thee an everlasting Covenant.

61. Then

61. Then thou shalt remember thy ways and be ashamed, when thou receive thy sisters, thy elder and thy younger: and I will give them to thee for daughters; but not by thy former Covenant.

62. And I will establish my Covenant with thee; and thou shalt know that I am the Lord.

63. That thou may remember and be confounded, and never open thy mouth any more because of thy shame, when I am pacified toward thee for all that thou hast done, says the Lord God.

Chap. XXXV. 11 v. For thus says the Lord God; Behold, I, even I, will both search for my sheep, and find them out.

12. As a shepherd gathers his flock in the day that his sheep are scattered, so will I seek out my sheep, and will deliver them from all places where they have been scattered, before the cloudy and dark day.

13. And I will bring them out from the people, and gather them from the countries, and will bring them to their own land and I will feed them on the mountains of Israel by the rivers, and make them inhabit the waste places of the country.

22. Therefore I will save my flock, and they shall be no more a prey; and I will judge between cattle and cattle.

23. And I will set up one shepherd over them, and he shall feed them even my servant David: he shall feed them, and he shall be their shepherd,

24. And I THE LORD (*meaning* CHRIST) will be their God, and my servant David (*meaning his descendant*) a Prince among them: I the Lord have spoken it.

Chap. XXXVI. 6 v. Prophesy, therefore, concerning the land of Israel, and say to the mountains, to the hills, to the rivers, and to the valleys, Thus says the Lord God; behold, I have spoken in my jealousy and fury, because ye have borne the shame of the heathen.

7. Therefore thus says the Lord God; I have lifted up my hand, surely the heathen that are about you shall bear their own shame.

8. But ye, O mountains of Israel, shall shoot forth your branches, and yield your fruit to my people of Israel: for they are at hand to come.

12. Yea, I will cause men to walk on you even my people Israel; and they shall possess thee, thou shalt be their inheritance, *and thou shalt no more henceforth bereave them of men.*

33. Thus says the Lord God; in the day that I clean you from all your iniquities, I will also cause you to dwell in the cities, and the waste places shall be built.

34. And the desolate land shall be tilled, which lay desolate in the sight of all that passed by:

35. And they shall say, This land that was desolate is become like the garden of Eden; and the waste, and desolate, and ruined cities, are fenced, and are full of inhabitants.

36. Then the heathen that are left round about you shall know, that I the Lord build the ruined places, and plant that which was desolate: I the Lord have spoken it, and will do it.

37. Thus says the Lord God; I will yet for this be enquired of by the House of Israel, to do it for them: I will encrease them with men like a flock.

38. As the holy flock, as the flock of Jerusalem in her solemn feasts; so shall the waste cities be filled with flocks of men: and they shall know that I am the Lord.

Chap. XXXVII. 20 v. And the sticks which thou write on shall be in thy hand before their eyes.

21. And say to them, Thus says the Lord God: behold, I will take the Children of Israel from among the Heathen, whither they are gone, and will gather them on every side, and bring them into their own land.

22. And I will make them One nation in the land upon the mountains of Israel, and there shall be One king to them all: they shall be no more two nations, neither shall they be divided into two kingdoms any more at all.

23. Neither shall they defile themselves any more with their idols, nor with their detestable things, nor with any of their transgressions: but I will save them out of all their dwelling places wherein they have sinned, and clean them; so shall they be my people, and I will be their God.

24. *And David my servant shall be King over them;* and they all shall have one shepherd: they shall also walk in my judgements, and observe my statutes to do them.

25. And they shall dwell in the land that I have given to Jacob my servant, in which your fathers have dwelt; and they shall dwell therein, *even they and their children, and children's children for ever*; and my Servant David (meaning his visible descendant) shall be their prince for ever.

The Vision of Ezekiel relative to Jerusalem, alludes to the grandeur and extent of it when rebuilt by the Jews after their return in the year of one thousand seven hundred and ninety-eight: it will be the CAPITAL OF THE WORLD, and from it will go once more to all nations the commands of the LIVING GOD.

The Prophet HOSEA, CHAP. II.

18. And in that day I will make a covenant for them with the beasts of the field, with the fowls of heaven, and with the creeping things of the ground: *and I will break the Bow, the Sword, and the Battle out of the Earth*; and they shall lie down with safety,

19. And I will betroth thee to me for ever; yea, I will betroth thee to me in righteousness and in truth, in loving kindness and in mercies.

20. I will even betroth thee to me with faithfulness, and thou shalt know the Lord.

23. And I will sow her to me in the earth, and I will have mercy on her that had not obtained mercy (*meaning Jerusalem*): and I will say to them which were not my people (*meaning the Jews during their dispersion*), YE ARE MY PEOPLE; and they shall say, THOU ART OUR GOD.

Chap. iii. 4. For the Children of Israel shall be many days without a King, and without a Prince, and without a Sacrifice, and without an Image, without an Ephod, and without Teraphim.

5. Afterwards the Children of Israel shall return and seek the Lord their God, and David their king; and they shall fear the Lord, *and shall know his goodness in the latter days.*

The Prophet JOEL, CHAP. III.

1. For behold, in those days, and in that time, *when I bring again the captivity of* Judah to Jerusalem.

2. I will also gather all nations, and bring them down to the valley of Jehoshaphat to plead with them there for my people, for Israel my heritage, whom they have scattered among the nations, and for dividing my land.

9. Proclaim ye this among the gentiles: prepare war, wake up the mighty men, let all the men of war draw near, let them come up.

10. Beat your ploughshares into swords, and your reaping-hooks into spears; let the weak say, I am strong.

11. Assemble yourselves and come, all ye heathen, gather yourselves together round about; thither cause thy mighty ones to come down, O Lord.

12. Let the heathen be waked, to come up to the valley of Jehoshaphat: for it is there I will sit to judge all the heaven round about.

14. Multitudes, multitudes in the valley of decision; for the day of the Lord is near in the valley of decision.

After the restoration of the Jews, the barbarous nations will send great armies to invade their lands, God will permit them to advance, that he may destroy them with his fire from heaven.

15. The SUN and MOON shall be darkened, and the STARS shall withdraw their shining.

16. The Lord will roar out from Zion, and utter his voice from Jerusalem; the heavens and the earth shall shake, but the Lord will be the hope of his people, and the strength of the children of Israel.

17. So ye shall know that I am the LORD GOD (*directed to all nations*) dwelling in Zion my holy mountain; then shall Jeru-

Jerusalem be holy, and there shall no strangers pass through her any more.

18. And it shall come to pass in that day that the mountains shall drop down new wine, and the hills shall flow with milk, and all the rivers of Judah shall flow with waters, and a fountain shall come forth, from the house of the Lord, and water the valley of Shittim.

19. Egypt shall be a desolation, and Edom, a desolate wilderness, for their violence against the children of Judah, and for shedding their innocent blood in the land.

20. But Judah shall dwell for ever, and Jerusalem from generation to generation.

21. For I will cleanse their blood that I have not cleansed; for the Lord dwells in Zion.

The Prophet AMOS. CHAP. IX.

8. Behold the eyes of the Lord God are upon the sinful kingdom; and I will destroy it from the face of the earth; but I will not utterly destroy the house of Jacob, says the Lord.

9. For lo, I will command, and I will sift the house of Israel from among all nations, like corn sifted in a sieve, yet the least grain shall not fall upon the earth.

10. All the sinners of my people shall die by the sword, which say the evil shall not overtake nor prevent us.

11. IN THAT DAY, I will raise up the Tabernacle of David that is fallen, *(meaning the restoration of his descendant to the government of the Children of Israel)* and close up the breaches thereof; and I will raise up his ruins, and build it as in the days of old.

12. That they may possess the remnant of Edom, and of all the heathen which are not called by my name, says the Lord, who does this.

13. Behold the days will come, says the Lord, that the Plowman shall overtake the Reaper, and the Treader of grapes him that sows the seed; the mountains shall drop sweet wine, and all the hills shall flow with milk.

14. And I will bring again the captivity of my people of Israel; they shall build the waste cities, and inhabit them; they shall plant vineyards, and drink the wine of them; they shall also make gardens, and eat the fruit of them.

15. And I will plant them upon their own land; they shall no more be pulled up out of their own land which I have given them, says the Lord thy God.

The Prophet OBADIAH. CHAP. I.

8. Shall I not in that day, says the Lord, even destroy the wise men out of Edom, and understanding out of the Mount of Esau.

9. And

9. And thy mighty men, O Teman, shall be dismayed, to the end that every one of the Mount of Esau may be cut off by slaughter.

10. For thy violence against thy brother Jacob, shame shall cover thee, and thou shalt be cut off for ever.

15. For the day of the Lord is near upon all the heathen: as thou hast done, it shall be done to thee; thy reward shall return on thy own head.

16. For as ye have drunk on my holy mountain, (meaning the Turks) so shall all the heathen drink continually; yea, they shall drink and swallow down, and they shall be as though they had not been.

17. But upon MOUNT ZION shall be deliverance, and on it shall be holiness: for the house of Jacob shall possess all their possessions.

18. And the house of Jacob shall be a fire, and the house of Joseph a flame, and the house of Esau for stubble: they shall kindle in them and devour them; there shall not be any remaining of the house of Esau: for the Lord has spoken it.

19. And they of the South shall possess the Mount of Esau; and they of the Plain, the Philistines: they shall possess their fields, and Ephraim the fields of Samaria, and Benjamin shall possess Gilead:

20. And the captivity of this host of the children of Israel, shall possess that of the Canaanites, even to Zeruphath, and the captivity of Jerusalem, which is in Sepharad, shall possess the cities of the South.

21. And Saviours shall come up on Mount Zion to judge the Mount of Esau; and then THE KINGDOM SHALL BE THE LORD's.

The Turks are descended from Esau, the brother of Jacob; but their Emperor, and his family, *are descended from Jonathan, the Son of Saul, King of Israel.*—Told me by Revelation.

The Prophet MICAH, CHAP. IV.

1. But in the last days it shall come to pass, that the Mountain of the House of the Lord shall be established on the top of the mountains; it shall be exalted above the hills, and people shall flow to it.

6. In that day, says the Lord, I will assemble her that has halted, and I will gather her that was driven out, and her that I have afflicted.

7. And I will make the remnant that halted, and her that was cast far off, a strong nation; and the Lord will reign over them in Mount Zion, from henceforth, even for ever.

The Prophet NAHUM, CHAP. I.

15. Behold upon the mountains the feet of him that brings good tidings, that publishes Peace! O Judah, keep thy solemn feasts and

and perform thy vows; *for the wicked shall no more pass through thee;* they are entirely cut off.

† The beginning of this verse means Chrift preaching the Gofpel of peace; the latter part, when the Jews are eftablifhed at Jerufalem after their next reftoration.

The Prophet ZEPHANIAH, CHAP. III.

13. The remnant of Ifrael fhall not commit iniquity, nor fpeak lies, neither fhall a deceitful tongue be found in their mouth; for they fhall feed and lie down, and none fhall make them afraid.

14. Sing, O daughter of Zion; fhout, O Ifrael; be glad and rejoice with all thy heart, O daughter of Jerufalem.

15. The Lord has taken away thy Judgments; he has caft out thy Enemy: THE KING OF ISRAEL, even the Lord, is in the midft of thee; *thou fhalt not fee evil any more.*

16. In that day it fhall be faid to Jerufalem, Fear thou not; and to Zion, Let not thy hands be flack.

17. The Lord thy God in the midft of thee is mighty; he will fave, and rejoice over thee with joy; he will reft in his love, and rejoice over thee with finging.

18. I will gather them that are forrowful for the folemn affemblies who are of thee, to whom the reproach of thee was a burthen.

19. Behold, at that time I will undo all which afflicts thee; and I will fave her that is ftopped, and gather her that was driven out; *and I will get them praife and renown* in every land where they have been put to fhame.

20. At the time that I bring you again, even the time when I gather you; *for I will get you a name, and make you to be praifed among all the people of the earth,* when I turn away your captivity from before your eyes, fays the Lord.

The Prophet HAGGAI, CHAP. II.

20. And again the word of the Lord came to Haggai, in the four and twentieth day of the month, faying,

21. Speak to Zerubbabel, governor of Judah, and fay, I will fhake the heavens and the earth;

22. And I will overthrow the *Thrones of Kingdoms,* and I will deftroy the ftrength of the *Kingdoms of the Heathen:* I will overthrow their Chariots, and thofe that ride in them; their Horfes and Riders fhall come down, *every one by the fword of the other.*

The time alluded to by the prophet is that which is immediately before the reftoration of the Jews, in the latter days of the world: the prefent is it.

23. In that day, fays the Lord of Hofts, I will take thee, O ZERUBBABEL my fervant, the fon of Shealtiel, and will
make

make thee as a fignet; for I have chofen thee, fays the Lord of Hofts.

The meaning of this verfe is, that when the former part of this prophecy is fulfilling, Zerubbabel will be revived in his defcendant, who will be, *like himfelf, the vifible Prince and Governor of the Jews;* the time is nearly come for this man to be openly revealed, and to have in all other refpects this very gracious, and very wonderful promife from God fulfilled.

The Prophet ZACHARIAH, CHAP. VIII.

7. Thus fays the Lord of Hofts, Behold, I will fave my people from the Eaft country, and from the Weft country:

8 And I will bring them, and they fhall dwell in the midft of Jerufalem; they fhall be my people, and I will be their God, in truth and in righteoufnefs.

Chap. x. 6. And I will ftrengthen the houfe of Judah, and I will fave the houfe of Jofeph, and I will bring them again to replace them; for I will have mercy on them, *and they fhall be as if I had not caft them off; for I am the Lord their God,* and I will hear them.

7. And they of Ephraim fhall be like a mighty man, and their hearts fhall rejoice as through wine; yea, their children fhall fee it and be glad; their hearts fhall rejoice in the Lord.

8. I will hifs for them and gather them; for I have redeemed them, and they fhall increafe as they have increafed.

9. And I will fow them among the people; and they fhall remember me in far countries, and they fhall live with their children, and turn again.

10. I will bring them again alfo out of the land of Egypt, and gather them out of Affyria; and I will bring them into the land of Gilead, and Lebanon, and place fhall not be found for them.

Chap. xii. 1. The burthen of the word of the Lord for Ifrael, fays the Lord, who ftretches out the heavens, and lays the foundations of the earth, that forms the fpirit of man within him.

2. Behold, I will make Jerufalem a cup of trembling to all the people round about, when they fhall be in the fiege both againft Judah and againft Jerufalem.

3. And in that day I will make Jerufalem a burthenfome ftone for all people; all that burthen themfelves with it fhall be cut in pieces, though all the people of the earth be gathered together againft it.

4. In that day, fays the Lord, I will fmite every horfe with aftonifhment, and his rider with madnefs: and I will open my eyes upon the houfe of Judah, and I will ftrike every horfe of the people with blindnefs.

5. And

5. And the governors of Judah shall say in their heart, the inhabitants of Jerusalem shall be our strength in the Lord of Hosts, our God.

6. In that day I will make the Governors of Judah like a hearth of fire among wood, like a torch of fire in a sheaf; they shall devour all the people round about, on the right hand and on the left, and Jerusalem shall be inhabited again, even Jerusalem in her own place.

7. The Lord also will save the Tents of Judah first, to preserve the distinction of the house of David, that the inhabitants of Jerusalem may not exalt themselves against Judah.

8. In that day the Lord will defend the inhabitants of Jerusalem; and he that is feeble among them in that day shall be as David, and the house of David shall be as God—as the angel of the Lord before them.

This prophecy means the same time and the same invasion of Judah by the heathen, as that mentioned by the prophet Joel in the third chapter, which is explained already.

9. And it shall come to pass in that day, that I will destroy the people of all the nations which are come against Jerusalem.

10. And I will pour upon the house of David, and upon the inhabitants of Jerusalem, the spirit of grace and of supplications; and they shall look to me that was pierced, and shall mourn like him that mourns for his only son; and they shall be in bitterness like him that is in bitterness for his first born.

11. In that day there shall be great mourning in Jerusalem, like the mourning of Hadadrimon in the valley of Megiddon.

12. And the land shall mourn, every family apart: the family of the house of David apart, and their wives apart; the family of Nathan apart, and their wives apart,

13. The family of the house of Levi apart, and their wives apart; the family of Shimei apart, and their wives apart.

14. All the families that remain, every family apart, and their wives apart.

When the heathen armies invade the land of Israel, it will be with a resolution to seize on every moveable thing and destroy the people; the Jews then acknowledging the MESSIAH as GOD, will believe under an excess of grief that he was crucified; sensible of their perilous condition, and knowing that it is he only can save them, they will, every man and family implore him for compassion and deliverance.

The HEBREWS will be delivered, and the HEATHEN entirely destroyed.

The Prophet MALACHI, CHAP. IV.

5. Behold, I will send you ELIJAH the Prophet before the coming of the *great and dreadful day* of the Lord;

6. And

6. And he shall turn the heart of the fathers to the children, and the heart of the children to their fathers; left I come and smite the earth with a curse.

The great Prophet alluded to in this chapter, is the same that will be revealed to the Jews to order their return to Jerusalem *before the expiration of One thousand seven hundred and ninety-eight;* he will possess the spirit of God, and the power of fire, equal to Elijah; he will make known the judgments of God, that all nations may be benefited, and may endeavour to survive them when they are commanded to be fulfilled.

The alterations I have made in copying some of the Prophecies, is by the direction and command of the Lord God.

THE JUDGMENTS OF GOD.

The very loud and unusual kind of Thunder that was heard in the beginning of January, 1791, was the voice of the Angel mentioned in the Eighteenth chapter of the Revelation, proclaiming the judgment of God and the fall of Babylon the great; it was the loudest that ever was heard since man was created, and shook the whole earth every time the angel spoke; it roared through the trees, and made a noise over London like the falling of mountains of stones.

Many buildings were damaged at the time of this thunder, and many persons were frightened by it; the great flashes of lightning proceeded also from the angel, and was, according to the first verse, reflected from the brightness of his glory.

REVELATION to St. JOHN, CHAP. XVIII.

1. And after these things I saw another Angel come down from heaven, having great power: and the Earth was lightened with his glory.

2. And he cried mightily with a strong voice, *(meaning the thunder)* saying, BABYLON THE GREAT is fallen, is fallen, &c.

3. For all nations have drunk of the wine of the wrath of her fornication, and the kings of the earth have committed fornication with her, and the merchants of the earth are waxed rich through the abundance of her delicacies.

4. And I heard another voice from heaven, saying, *Come out of her, my people,* that ye be not partakers of her sins, and that ye receive not of her plagues.

5. For her sins have reached up to heaven, and God hath remembered her iniquities.

6. Reward her, even as she rewarded you, and double to her double, according to her works; in the Cup which she has filled, fill to her double.

7. How much she hath glorified herself and lived deliciously, so much torment and sorrow give her; *for she says in her heart,* I sit a QUEEN, and am no Widow, and shall see no sorrow.

8. Therefore shall her Plagues come in one day, death, and

mourning, and famine, *and she shall be utterly burnt with fire;* for strong is he Lord God who judges her.

The Lord God was so exceeding angry at the time of the loud thunder I have mentioned in the preceding par., that he determined to leave his other Judgments unfulfilled relative to London, and burn her immediately with fire from Heaven: soon afterwards I was informed by Revelation of what the thunder meant, and was commanded to go from London beyond the distance of eighteen miles. I had, *similar to the prophet Daniel at Babylon,* an attending Angel to explain all the Visions, and support me under the grief I was loaded with for it's approaching fall.

The Lord God knowing that I loved him with all my heart, and had often resisted the calls of hunger and distress, rather than comply with customs that would offend him, pitied me; for I had beseeched him to let me inform the people of London of their danger, and try by all possible means to save them, but was refused permission, because they would imprison and use me very ill for it.

In addition to all that God had promised and repeated by his angel to make me happy, he was now pleased to give me another proof of his unalterable regard, and convince me by it, that *although he could not in justice to his recorded judgment spare London,* yet for my sake he would shew mercy to some; and take care, that by sickness and other causes, to remove the persons I desired should be saved, to a sufficient distance beyond the limits to be destroyed and sunk.

After thanking the Lord God, I mentioned several, both men and women, and called the remembrance of his mercy to others whose names I did not know; but pointed them out in my mind.

Among those I mentioned, was William Pultney, William Pitt, Gilbert Elliot, Charles Grey, the Earl of Buckinghamshire, the Marquis of Lansdown, the Earl of Chatham, Maitland, now called Earl of Lauderdale; Henry Phipps, for I remember his brother to have done me an act of friendship; John Dalrymple, John Griffin Griffin, Alderman Pickett, *because that during his Mayoralty he opposed by a public advertisement the frequency of taking oaths;* in doing so he honoured that all remembering God, who will in due time as publicly honor him for it. Wilberforce, Bastard, Sheridan, Philip Stevens, Charles Fox: John Luke, a poor Quaker; Samuel Hood; the King and his family, for they were to be gathered into London; Ponsonby, for whom I conceived an esteem, from observing in his countenance openness and honesty, and possessing as I thought, a heart similar to my own, I was led to entreat for him: until last year I could assign no other reason for mentioning that name than what I have given; but the true one is, that as God had determined not only to keep in London the people then in it, but likewise to allow great multitudes to be

drawn

drawn to it from all parts of the country, he would be found among the number to be deſtroyed; for which to prevent his death in ſuch a place, the Lord God influenced me to regard him, that I might afterwards remember ſuch a perſon and be mindful of his ſafety.

I am not in the leaſt acquainted with the man I have mentioned, whom God was pleaſed to diſtinguiſh by ſo great a teſtimony of his regard, but although I am not, and our names are differei.;, *he is—as well as myſelf;* deſcended from DAVID, KING OF ISRAEL. The Counteſs of Buckinghamſhire, whom I am no more acquainted with than the ſtranger I have mentioned before, is likewiſe deſcended from David, King of Iſrael: the family ſhe is married into are alſo of the Hebrews, and are deſcended from JOSEPH the once Preſident of Egypt.

There are many families of the ſame origin as thoſe three I have named, made known to me by revelation, but I am forbid to mention any of them at preſent for public knowledge.

After entreating for the perſons I have ſet down, and pointing from my mind to numbers beſides whoſe names I did not know, I was, *to prepare me for the deſignation of God*, carried up to heaven in a viſion, and ſaw on my right ſide at a ſmall diſtance, a beautiful ſilver white bird in the ſhape of a Dove, but a little larger; it was the HOLY GHOST, and was the very ſame that deſcended on the head of my BLESSED SAVIOUR, when he came up from being baptized in the river Jordan; he kept between me and *Satan*, who was then revealed that I might witneſs it, and great power given him to viſit the Earth. The LORD GOD then ſpoke to me from the middle of a white ſhining cloud.

After this I was in a Viſion, *Having the Angel of God near me*, and ſaw Satan walking leiſurely in.o London, his face had a ſmile, but under it his looks were ſly, crafty, and deceitful. On the right ſide of his forehead were ſeven dark ſpots; he was dreſſed in White and Scarlet Robes.

Again I was in a Viſion and ſaw London a ſcene of confuſion, it was effected on a ſudden; all the People were armed and appeared quite furious: I was carried through the City in the Spirit of God to ſee all things that were deſigned ſhould come to paſs, and be informed how quick they could be accompliſhed.

After this I was in a Viſion, and ſaw a large river run through London coloured with human Blood.

Exceedingly unhappy for all that I ſaw, and which I knew would ſoon be fulfilled, I prayed and entreated the Lord God to give me one more inſtance of his mighty regard, *by ſparing London and the great multitude in it*. I ſaid, I acknowledge, O Lord my God, that the People do very wrong, but it is through compulſion and for want of knowing better.

The Lord God was ſo highly diſpleaſed, that I ſhould after all his former kindneſs ſtrain his affection and entreat him to annul his *Recorded Judgment*, as to ſtop me, and in a voice of great ſharpneſs and anger ſay, *They have my bleſſed Goſpel, and will not obey*

obey it. The Angel that was appointed to give me inſtruction forſook me in an inſtant on hearing this anſwer. I trembled for my life, and ſeemed to be another man; for I was afraid of being deſtroyed with the City. It was three days after this before the Lord God would be reconciled to hear my prayers, and ſpeak to me with his former kindneſs.

In ten days after the three I was in a Viſion, and being carried up to heaven, the Lord God ſpoke to me from the middle of a large white cloud, and ſaid in a ſtrong clear voice—ALL, ALL. I pardon London, and all the people in it, for your ſake: there is no other man on earth that could ſtand before me to aſk for ſo great a thing.

For ever, O Lord my God, I will praiſe and thank you for this great inſtance of your bleſſed regard; all Nations will hear it, and may all Nations honour you by their obedience: your great mercy is over them all, and by its goodneſs the world is now ſafe.

Had London been deſtroyed in the year of 1791, the place where it ſtands would have formed a great Bay or Inlet of the channel; all the land between Windſor and the Downs would have been ſunk, including a diſtance of eighteen miles each ſide, but conſiderably more towards the ſea coaſt; it would be ſunk to the depth of ſeventy fathoms, or four hundred and twenty feet, that no traces of the City might be ever found, or even ſo much as looked for.

21. And A MIGHTY ANGEL took up a ſtone, *like a great millſtone*, and caſt it into the Sea, ſaying, Thus with violence ſhall that great City Babylon be thrown down, *and ſhall be found no more at all.*

That all men of wiſdom and diſcernment may underſtand, on reading the Revelation, that there are Two Cities mentioned in it *Spiritually* under the names of Babylon the Great, I will aſſiſt them by clearly marking out the diſtinction.

ROME, the SPIRITUAL BABYLON, mentioned in the ſeventeenth chapter, is deſcribed in the third verſe, *to be away into the wilderneſs;* meaning by the words into the Wilderneſs, that the City is ſituated *Inland.*

But LONDON, the SPIRITUAL BABYLON alſo, mentioned in the eighteenth chapter, is deſcribed by St. John *as the greateſt Sea Port,* for Ships, Wealth, and Commerce, in the World.

11. And the Merchants of the Earth ſhall weep and mourn over her; for no man buyeth her merchandize any more.

12. The merchandize of Gold, and Silver, and precious Stones, and of Pearls, and fine Linen, and Purple, and Silk, and Scarlet, and all Thyine Wood, and all manner of Veſſels of Ivory, and all manner of veſſels of moſt precious Wood, and of Braſs, and Iron, and Marble:

13. And Cinnamon, and Odours, and Ointments, and Frankincenſe, and Wine, and Oil, and fine Flour, and Wheat, and Beaſts,

Beasts, and Sheep, and Horses, and Chariots, and *Slaves*, and *Souls of Men*.

14. And the Fruits that thy Soul lusted after are departed from thee, and all things which were dainty and goodly are departed from thee, *and thou shalt find them no more at all*.

15. The Merchants of these things, who were made rich by her, shall stand afar off for the fear of her torment, weeping and wailing.

16. And saying, Alas, alas, that GREAT CITY, that was cloathed in fine Linen, and Purple, and Scarlet, and decked with gold and precious Stones, and Pearls! *For in one hour, such great Riches is come to nought*.

17. And every Ship-master, and all the company in Ships, and Sailors, *and as many as trade by Sea*, stood afar off.

18. And cried, *when they saw the smoke of her burning*, saying, What City is like to this great City!

19. And they cast dust on their heads, and cried, weeping and wailing, saying, Alas, alas, that great City; *wherein were made rich all that had Ships in the Sea*, by reason of her costliness : for in one hour is she made desolate.

20. Rejoice over her, THOU HEAVEN, and ye HOLY APOSTLES and PROPHETS; for GOD hath avenged you on her.

Read attentively the Eighteenth Chapter, and you will perceive described in it, the prodigious wealth, grandeur, and commerce of London; then remember that the very great Thunder, and Lightning, I have mentioned, was in the depth of Winter, *an unusual time of year for the like;* but they were as St. John exactly describes them in the first and second verses. Meditate on these things, weigh them attentively in your mind, and all I have wrote besides; and the Spirit of God, if you love Wisdom, will enlighten your understanding to see, and will also strike you with a Conviction of their truth.

―――

The following would have been the condition of England, which the Lord God shewed me in the month of July 1791, had his judgement of desolation on the world been suddenly fulfilled at the appointed time in 1793.

I was in a VISION, and was carrried away by the SPIRIT of God to a field of young wheat, which was grown about four inches high from the ground; an elderly English woman stood by me; *she had no covering on her head*, but over her arms was an old black silk cloak; it was worn threadbare, and rent in many places.—While I was observing the dress and poverty of the woman, the wheat sprung up in an instant, and shot out to the size of full ears, the largest I ever saw in my life: astonished at such a sight, and wondering what it should mean, I stooped to feel some with my hand; when I had, *the woman looked down*

down to me with a countenance expressive of great distress to implore my pity and assistance, then turned her face away to the East, and afterwards looked up to heaven, as if she wanted Rain and a cool Wind.

After this I cast my eyes over the surface of the land; it was scorched to a dark brown, and frightful to look at; I could see no Grass in the Meadows, and the Bushes in the hedges were all burnt brown, so great and mighty was the heat; I could see no Beasts in the fields, and the Fowls of heaven were all flown away.

The judgment of desolation being suspended, is the reason that this vision of Famine and Distress is also. When it takes place, England, like the woman and her cloak, *(for she was an allusion to this country)* will be very poor, worn out, and rent in many places.

After this I was in a Vision, and saw a large SWORD unsheathed in heaven: soon after I saw a large CUP full of red wine, and much froth on the top, lifted up and held out to all nations.

THE JUDGMENT OF DESOLATION ON ALL NATIONS.

The THUNDER that was heard in the evening of the third of August, 1793, was the voice of the Angel mentioned in the nineteenth chapter of the Revelation standing in the Sun.

17. And I saw an Angel standing in the sun; and he cried with a loud voice, *(meaning the thunder)* saying to all the fowls that fly in the midst of Heaven, Come and gather yourselves together to the supper of the great God;

18. That ye may eat the flesh of *Kings*, and the flesh of *Captains*, and the flesh of *mighty men*, and the flesh of horses, and of them that sit on them, *and the flesh of all men*, both free and bond, both small and great.

The dead will increase so fast, and be in such prodigious numbers, when this judgment takes place, that the living will not be sufficient to bury them, but will leave the bodies exposed to the fowls of heaven for meat.

The flashes of Lightning which issued during the thunder, proceeded from the Glory of the Angel proclaiming the judgment of God, and resembled in colour THE CLEAR DAY LIGHT.

The *Second Thunder* that gave notice of God's approaching judgment, was on Wednesday evening, the 7th of August, 1793, *as is mentioned in the seventh of the Revelation*, and was the voice of the Angel ascending from the East, having the Seal of the living God.

2. And I saw another Angel ascending from the East, having the SEAL of the LIVING GOD; and he cried with a loud voice *(the thunder)* to the *Four Angels*, to whom it was given to hurt the Earth and the Sea;

3. Saying,

3. Saying, Hurt not the earth, neither the sea, nor the trees, till we have sealed the servants of our God in their foreheads.

The flashes of lightning, which issued during the time of this thunder, proceeded likewise from the Glory of the Angel, and resembled in colour FINE AMBER.

The next and last THUNDER, *if the judgement had not been suspended for my sake*, would be on the eleventh of August following, and would have been, according to the sixteenth chapter of the Revelation, the fourth Angel pouring out his Vial on the Sun.

8. And the fourth Angel poured out his Vial on the Sun, and power was given him to scorch men with fire.

9. And men were scorched with great heat, and blasphemed the name of God who has power over these plagues; and they repented not to give him glory.

The flashes of lightning during this thunder, which would continue many hours, would likewise proceed from the glory of the Angel, and would be in strength and colour LIKE THE BURNING FLAME.

This thunder would be accompanied by a violent storm of large HAIL STONES, which, with the lightning would kill multitudes of people and destroy the Harvest in many countries.

Soon after this thunder, *the short time of four days only*, the judgment of God on the world would begin to be fulfilled. The winds would be suspended in the Firmament, *according to the seventh chapter*, that breathing might almost cease; the great body of heat that would immediately after be poured down from Heaven on the earth, *would be so fierce and powerful as to move the world, and kill every living thing, both man and beast, exposed under it in the open air.* The trees, bushes in the hedges, grass in the meadows, and what corn was left from the hail, would be cut off and destroyed by this great and mighty heat. Most of the Ships would be destroyed at sea, and all the fish near the surface killed. Millions of the human race would die in all nations from this burning heat, and the many plagues it would produce.

The *Nineteenth, Seventh, Sixteenth, Sixth, Eighth, and Fourteenth Chapters*, mean the same time, the same things, and are as one chapter to fulfil the judgement of God.

The fifteenth of August, 1793, was the time appointed by the Lord God to fulfil the parts of the Revelation I have mentioned, and punish the world with desolation; but from HIS GREAT MERCY and regard for Me, that I may be esteemed in this Country, and by all others when I am revealed, suspended this judgement for a Time: it hangs, however, over all nations.

Look at the age of the world, read attentively the chapters I have mentioned, with what I have wrote besides; and you will discover in your own breast a Light, to see and believe by.

That LIGHT *I mean* which is often called *a certain something*, an *internal monitor*, that applauds man for courting wisdom,—for being just, and doing good: but that never fails to reproach him for embracing folly, and doing evil: it is indeed no other than the SPIRIT of the LIVING GOD.

All the Prophecies given in Visions from God are concealed from the knowledge of man by mysterious allusions until the proper time, and the appointed perfon for them to be revealed to. For it is not in the cunning of any man, even affifted by the wifdom of all the reft on earth, to fearch out the deep fecrets of God, or with truth to unfold the meaning of his vifions; *they are wonderful*, they cannot be difcovered until God himfelf pleafes to remove the Covering of fecrecy, and, through an appointed perfon, bleffes the world with a knowledge of their true meaning.

The fulfilling of the judgements of God, however deftructive they may prove to the Governments and Nations which they are directed againft, are not allowed to affect my perfonal fafety, nor operate in the leaft to my prejudice: for the certainty of my elevation to the greateft *Principality* that ever will be in the world, cannot be prevented by the rife or fall of any human power on earth; becaufe it is the repeated Covenant of God to my forefathers, and his facred promife now by Revelation to myfelf.

The obfcurity of David was no objection with a difcerning God to make him the MONARCH OF ISRAEL, and afterwards promife the fucceffion to his Family for ever; neither is mine now to his fulfilling that promife, and holding me up to the world as the vifible Governor of the Jews. For all the works of God are wonderful, and very far exceed the capacity of man to know, where they begin, how they are directed, on whom, or which way they will end: I that have more knowledge of them, and of futurity revealed to me, than any other under the whole heaven, obferve the operation of every new one with more amazement than the former.

Therefore my prefent poverty is no obftacle to my future Elevation, neither is it of much concern to myfelf; for the time of my being revealed with power from Heaven is nigh; when God, to manifeft his regard, will give me favour with many, and influence all the people of London to help me.

I am the Prophet that will be revealed to the Jews to order their departure from all Nations to go to the Land of Ifrael, their own country, in a fimilar manner to Mofes in Egypt, but with additional power.

I was an Officer in the Englifh Navy, and neceffarily fo, although I did not know it, that the judgement of God on David, king of Ifrael, might be fulfilled, which was, that the Sword fhould never depart from his Houfe.

It is fifteen hundred years fince my family was feparated from the Jews, and loft all knowledge of its origin; the laft on record in the Scripture, is JAMES: 13th chap. 55th ver. of St. Matthew. *Told me by Revelation.*

The Government of the Jewifh Nation will, *under the Lord God,* be committed to me, that the everlafting covenant from him to David may be manifefted in the vifible Prince and Governor of the Jews.

Second of SAMUEL CHAP. VII.

16. And thy HOUSE and thy KINGDOM, fhall be eftablifhed for ever before thee; thy THRONE fhail be eftablifhed for ever.

17. According to all thefe words, and according to all this Vifion, fo did Nathan fpeak to David.

JERE-

JEREMIAH, CHAP. XXXIII.

17. For thus says the Lord: David shall never want a Man to sit on the Trone of the House of Israel.

19. And the word of the Lord came to Jeremiah, saying,

20. Thus says the Lord, If ye can break my covenant of the Day, and my covenant of the Night, and that there should not be Day and Night in their Season;

21. Then may also my covenant be broke with David my servant, *that he should not have a Son to reign upon his Throne:* and with the Levites the priests my ministers.

22. As the host of Heaven cannot be numbered, neither the sand of the sea measured; so will I multiply the seed of David my servant, and the Levites that minister to me.

23. Moreover the word of the Lord came to Jeremiah saying,

24. Considerest thou not what this people have spoken, saying, The two families which the Lord has chosen, he has even cast them off. Thus they have despised my people, that they should be no more a nation before them.

25. *Thus says the LORD,* If my covenant be not with day and night, and if I have not appointed the ordinances of heaven and earth,

26. Then I will cast away the seed of Jacob, and David my servant, *so that I will not take any of his seed to be rulers over the seed of* ABRAHAM, ISAAC, and JACOB: for I will cause their captivity to return, and have mercy on them.

A knowledge of the Scripture, the Prophecies I have mentioned, and all that I have wrote besides, have been communicated to me through visions and revelations from the Lord God: the Prophet Daniel, and St. John, the Apostle, were instructed in the same manner to write what they have.

It is by the saving of Multitudes;—by Revealing, not only a true Interpretation of the Prophecies, but also a Knowledge of the times, and those secret Parts of the Scripture which are not made known to any other Man under Heaven, that the Lord God begins with announcing to the World a Knowledge of his mighty Judgements, *The return of his former Mercy to the Hebrews,* their speedy Restoration to JERUSALEM, and the Rise of a FAVOURITE FAMILY.

RICHARD BROTHERS.

LONDON, No. 57, Paddington-street,
3d of the Month called JANUARY, 1794.

REVELATION TO St. JOHN, CHAP. XVII.

or

ROME.

1 v. AND there came one of the seven angels, which had the seven Vials, and talked with me, saying to me, Come hither, and I will shew thee the Judgment of the Great whore, *(meaning Rome,)* that sits upon many Waters, *(meaning her Government over many Nations.)*

2. With whom the Kings of the Earth have committed Fornication *(meaning, they have been seduced to imitate her evil practices,)* and the Inhabitants of the Earth have been made drunk with the wine of her fornication *(meaning they are likewise deluded to drink deep to a state of insensibility from her vain doctrines.)*

A remarkable instance of this was very lately practised, and really fulfilled at Naples; which, although governed by a King, is notwithstanding in the See of Rome, and about sixty miles distant. In consequence of a violent irruption of fire out of Mount Vesuvius, which is but a few miles from Naples, the similitude of a human head, called St. Januarius's—was carried in Procession, lifted up, and held out, fully believing that by honouring the Saint, through even this small part of his image, he himself in heaven, would be influenced to intercede with God to stop the great Rivers of fire which issued from the burning Mountain.

For a People, calling themselves Christians, which have had the Revelation so long to warn, and the blessed Gospel so long to instruct them, to embrace at this late hour of the world such an act of Superstition and Delusion, is indeed astonishing. But it is a part of that great chain of errors—still continued, which the Roman Government at a former period most wickedly bound its people in all nations; but Clergy in particular with; and which is plainly foretold by St. Paul in the fourth chapter of his first Epistle to Timothy, 1 ver. Now the Spirit *(which is the Holy Ghost)* speaks expressly that in the latter times some shall depart from the faith, giving heed to Seducing Spirits and Doctrines of Devils:

2. Speaking Lies in hypocrisy, having their consciences seared with a hot iron:

3. Forbidding to marry, &c.

The Papal Authority does not allow its Clergy to marry, from a belief that a man, by living in a state of separation from a woman, is better qualified to fulfil the duties of a Priest more acceptably to God, than a man that is a Husband and Father. Such doctrine is an evident proof to every discerning person that there is a great departure—or falling away from the true Faith: to continue then in the practice, after it is explained and made public by Divine command, is preferring darkness to light, the doctrines of Devils to the good words of God: it is giving a willing heed to the seduc-

cing

cing Spirits that St. Paul alludes to. Chrift, the Saviour of the World, who left his Gofpel of the Kingdom of Peace for the direction of all men, never made any fuch diftinction: for fome of his Apoftles were married, and fome were not: and he, as God the Father in the beginning of the Creation bleffed Adam and Eve, faying to them, "Be fruitful and multiply, and replenifh the Earth," &c. Repeating the fame after the Flood to Noah and his Sons: he never ordered, nor never intended, the cruel impofition of Celibacy on his immediate fervants—or any other defcription of men.

It is alfo an abomination to him; becaufe inconfiftent with the defign of his Creation, that any defcription of women under the vain pretence of what is falfely called Religion and Piety—of leading a more holy life—of ferving God better, fhould be fhut up for ever in Monafteries—inhumanly deprived of becoming Wives and Mothers.

I am commanded to fay, it is grievous and forrowful to the Lord God to fee Nations which acknowledge him, and which have the whole Scripture to inform them of his will, paying a blind—an Idolatrous obedience to human Ordinances, fupported by bad Oaths, and finful Vows, in direct oppofition to what he defigns, and what in the beginning the Covenant of his Bleffing prefcribes.

The XVII. CHAP. of the Revelation continued.

3. So he carried me away in the Spirit into the Wildernefs, *(meaning into the Country, as if far inland from the Sea)* where I faw a Woman *(meaning Rome)* fit upon a fcarlet coloured Beaft *(meaning the Pope)* full of names of blafphemy, *(his titles)* having Seven heads *(alluding to the feven Hills on which the City ftands)* and Ten Horns *(meaning the Cardinals.)*

4. And the Woman was arrayed in Purple and Scarlet colour, and decked with Gold and precious Stones, and Pearls, having a golden Cup in her hand full of abominations, and Filthinefs of her Fornication.

5. And upon her Forehead was a name written, Myftery—Babylon the Great, the Mother of Harlots *(meaning that fhe as a Mother ftood expofed for corrupting with her evil doctrines many Cities to the condition of harlots)* and Abominations of the Earth.

6. And I faw the woman Drunk with the blood of the Saints, and with the blood of the Martyrs of Jefus; and when I faw her, I wondered greatly aftonifhed.

This Babylon the Great, this Mother of Harlots, means Rome; but is fpiritually called by thofe names as an allufion to her excefs of guilt as a Babylon, and corruption of doctrine as a Mother.

St. John mentions in the third verfe, that he was carried away into the Wildernefs to fee Rome; meaning by the words *into the Wildernefs,* that Rome the City he goes to look at is fituated inland: this defcription is given to make a diftinction between it and London, the maritime Babylon, full of Ships, Seamen, and Commerce, mentioned in the Eighteenth Chapter.

The Scarlet coloured Beaft full of names of Blafphemy, with feven heads and ten horns, means the Pope—in this chapter only, and not in any other part of the Revelation, is the Pope alluded to under any name—or under any fignification whatever:

neither

neither is Rome but in one part, which is in the Sixteenth chapter and middle of the nineteenth verse. The Pope in addition to his many names of blasphemy, likewise assumes the powers and prerogatives of God, calling himself, instead of his blessed Saviour, The SUPREME HEAD of the CHURCH: as such he pretends, for it is only pretension to deceive the Ignorant, to be infallible, and to pardon the commission of sin in others: again, as if sanctified by the Holy Ghost, and commanded immediately from God to impart freely his mighty blessing and his mighty spirit to whom he pleases, he ordains, as it is called, Bishops, laying hands on them, and saying at the same time, Receive the Holy Ghost; he likewise claims a pre-eminence of holiness in his person, and obedience to Christ in his actions, above all the rest of mankind.

There is no man spiritual that is not sanctified by the Holy Ghost, and no man is sanctified that teaches by his doctrines—or recommends by his prayers opposition to Christ the Saviour, and disobedience to his Gospel of Peace; for it is through and by Christ the blessed spirit is given that sanctifies, which every man that believes in him, and obeys his commands, may have—may partake of its blessing and sweets; some more, some less, in all things, and for all occasions, as the Lord himself judges proper; but it will be given to every man in such sufficiency as to make him abundant in knowledge, and teaching him clearly the ways of Salvation.

Man may give to man a Title, but it is God only that can make man spiritual; it is he and none else that can give the Holy Ghost, the Divine Spirit of Truth; all other givers among mankind, who say, "by the imposition of our hands Receive the Holy Ghost, whose sins thou dost forgive, they are forgiven, and whose sins thou dost retain, they are retained;" are but as so many false Christs—vain pretenders—blasphemously endeavouring to imitate the true One.

For a Man to attempt to do what the TRUE CHRIST only can, is attempting an imposition, and justly constitutes a False Christ. For a Man to kneel down to a man to receive the Holy Ghost and then going forth by the authority of this false Christ—teaching and preaching under the name of the true Christ, but in opposition to his commands,—deluded by an opinion that he is Spiritual, because his Human Maker imposed on him to believe so, when in reality he is not, constitutes a False Prophet.

Those are the kind of people that the Lord Jesus Christ alludes to in the 24th Chapter of St. Matthew, and warns the world to beware of.

There are many that Preach and write under the name of Christ, without being influenced by his Spirit, or commanded by his word; for which, Observe all you that love him, and read this book, that he will not give his blessed Spirit—which is indeed the Holy Ghost, to any man exalted in pride and living under names of blasphemy; praying for the success and aggrandizement of particular men in War, at the expence of ruin, and destruction to others. And yet the Pope, to impress the multitude round him with reverence and awe, is entitled Holiness, the Vicar of Christ, Successor to St. Peter, and is accounted infallible; all such names are an evident demonstration of pride and falsehood; and as such, he has

has neither holiness from Christ in his person, nor obedience to the Gospel of Truth in his actions.

It is for Blasphemy, Idolatry, Deceit, teaching rebellion against Christ, and for being a shedder of blood by war that the Pope is called in the Revelation from God, a scarlet coloured Beast; under that dreadful name, though knelt to as divine, and exalted to the height of Heaven by Titles, *he sinks down into perdition,*—he is a fallen man, and is adjudged by that already testimony of St. John; to suffer the punishment of everlasting fire.

7 v. And the Angel said to me, wherefore didst thou marvel? I will tell thee the mystery of the Woman, and of the Beast that carries her *(meaning that governs her)* which has the Seven heads, and Ten horns.

8. The beast that thou saw, was, and is not, and shall ascend out of the bottomless pit, and go into Perdition: and they that dwell on the Earth shall wonder, whose names were not written in the Book of Life, from the foundation of the World, when they behold the Beast that was, and is not, and yet is.

War, Oaths, Violence, and Bloodshed, being in opposition to the commands of Christ in his gospel of the Kingdom of Peace, they belong to Satan and his Government of Darkness.

St. MATTHEW, CHAP. IV.

8 v. Again the Devil takes him up to an exceeding high mountain, and shews him all the kingdoms of the World, and the glory of them;

9. And says to him, all these things I will give thee if Thou wilt fall down and worship me.

10. Then says JESUS to him, Get thee hence, Satan: For it is written, thou shalt worship the LORD THY GOD, and him only shalt thou serve.

The Popes having rose to what they are, and established their power by the sword, is the reason that God mentions in this part of the Revelation to St. John, the Beast—or Papal Authority, to ascend from the bottomless pit: in the beginning they were great military Princes, and governed with large armies; but latterly their power became weak, and their consequence small; yet notwithstanding, the vain titles, pageantry, and Military parade is still preserved and closely embraced by the present.

The XVII. CHAP. of the Revelation continued.

9 v. And here is the mind which has Wisdom. The seven Heads are seven mountains on which the woman sits.

The woman means Rome; and the seven mountains, or hills on which the city is built, are meant by St. John as the seven heads of the Pope.

10. And there are seven Kings; five are fallen, and one is, and the other is not yet come; and when he comes he must continue a short space.

These seven Kings mean seven powerful Military Popes: they are denominated Kings, because they were warlike men, and in other respects governed with the Sword like them.

11. And

11. And the Beast that was, and is not, even he is the eighth, is the same as the Seven, and goes into Perdition.

This means the last military Pope of Rome; for as the Popedom has rose by the Sword, by the Sword also it will fall; and the last Pope alluded to in this verse, as well as the first military one alluded to in the eighth verse, goes into perdition.

12. And the Ten Horns which thou saw, are Ten Kings, which have received no kingdom as yet, but receive power as Kings One hour with the beast.

13. These have one mind, and shall give their power and strength to the beast.

These two verses mean the Cardinals, who are compared to Kings in name, but not in power: they are great, but not independent; they have a great name, but no independent Sovereignty: they are called, like the German Electors to the Emperor, as is mentioned in the seventh chapter of Daniel, the Horns of the Beast; because they assist the Pope with their counsel and authority.

14. These shall make war with the Lamb, but the Lamb shall overcome them; for he is Lord of lords and King of kings; and they that are with him are called, and chosen, and faithful.

The Pope and Cardinals, by their Teaching, Practice, and Government, are in a state of opposition to Christ; that is, they practise and encourage, to support their form of Government, SWEARING and WAR, the two principal things which Christ, above all others, prohibits in the most positive terms. It is for this opposition to his commands in the Gospel, that they are represented as making war against him: they are permitted, through the patient suffering of God to do so, until he can bear no longer with their rebellion, when, to fulfil this Prophecy and his decreed Judgment, they will be entirely cut off. CHRIST, as Supreme Head of the Church, acknowledges no Religion but what he has taught by his Gospel, which is Christianity; for there is no kind of church but one, and that is visible man: it consists of one person as well as a whole congregation; of one just man in a room, as well as a million any where else; he came into the world to save Sinners, and Redeem them from the chains of eternal death: the blessed Gospel is the great Bond of his promises, now put into the hands of all men that will receive it for their instruction; for which, all that read or hear it ought to remember their Solemn Covenant in Baptism, and take care that on their part the terms of his Salvation are complied with. To do which Man must, to fulfil the design of his creation, endeavor to live long, and live happy; to do that, he must abolish War, and live in constant Peace: he must likewise abolish swearing of every kind, because it leads to falsehood and Perjury, and make the innocent words of Yes or No the solemn bond of his public truth.

The men that are called Preachers of Christianity, instead of assuming vain Titles and lofty Political Names, instead of assisting in any way at Councils of State, they ought to stand between Princes and War, between Men and Strife, between Nations and Bloodshed; they should be true teachers of the Gospel, and, like the immediate Disciples of their blessed Saviour, always the Ministers of Peace.

The

The GOSPEL. *St.* MATTHEW, CHAP. V.

9. Bleſſed are the Peace-makers, for they ſhall be called the Children of God.

Chap. vi. 7. But when ye pray, uſe not vain repetitions, *as the Heathen do:* for they think that they ſhall be heard for their much ſpeaking.

8. Be not ye therefore like to them; for your Father knows what things ye have need of before ye aſk him.

9. *After this manner* therefore pray ye, Our Father, who art in Heaven; hallowed be thy name:

10. Thy Kingdom come; *thy will be done on Earth* as it is in Heaven, &c.

The Kingdom of God, which is aſked for every time this form of prayer is ſaid, is to live in Peace and Righteouſneſs: the Government of God in Heaven is Peace, and his will is, that man on Earth ſhould have the ſame: it is prayed for every Sunday throughout Europe, and yet, to the bluſhing ſhame of man, in a minute after he forgets it, forſakes the Kingdom of Peace, and fervently prays to the ſame compaſſionate God to go forth with Fleets and Armies.

St. PAUL *to the* GALATIANS, CHAP. I.

2. Grace be to you, and Peace from God the Father, and from our Lord Jeſus Chriſt.

8. But though we, or an Angel from Heaven, preach any other Goſpel to you than that which we have preached to you, let him be Accurſed.

To prevent the deſtruction of man by War and Falſehood, CHRIST, who ſhed his blood for the Redemption of man, prohibits in the moſt plain, clear, and poſitive words, all kind of ſtrife that it ſhould not increaſe to War, and all kind of ſwearing that it ſhould not multiply into falſehood; theſe two evils enforced by Law, and encouraged by Religion, under the time of Chriſtianity, and in contradiction to the bleſſed Goſpel of Truth, are the two principal Fountains that deluge the world with Sin, and deprive Heaven of many.

St. MATTHEW, CHAP. V.

19. Whoſoever therefore ſhall break one of theſe leaſt commandments, and ſhall teach men ſo, he ſhall be called the leaſt in the Kingdom of Heaven; but whoſoever ſhall do and teach them, the ſame ſhall be called great in the Kingdom of Heaven.

33. Again, ye have heard that it has been ſaid by them of old time *(meaning the Teachers formerly under the Law)*, Thou ſhalt not forſwear thyſelf, but ſhall perform to the Lord thy Oath.

34. But I ſay to you, *Swear not at all;* neither by Heaven, for it is God's Throne;

35. Nor by the Earth, for it is his footſtool; neither by Jeruſalem, for it is the City of the Great King.

36. Neither muſt thou ſwear by thy head, becauſe thou cannot make one hair of it white or black.

F   37. But

37. But let your communication be Yea, yea; and Nay, nay; for whatsoever is more than these comes of Evil.

38. Ye have heard that it has been said, *(meaning under the Law by Moses)* an Eye for an Eye, and a Tooth for a Tooth:

39. But I say to you, that ye resist not evil, but whosoever shall smite thee on the right cheek, turn to him the other also.

43. Ye have heard that it has been said, Thou shalt love thy Neighbor, and hate thy enemy:

44. But I say to you, Love your enemies; bless them that curse you; do good to them that hate you, and pray for them which despitefully use you, and persecute you.

45. That ye may be the children of your Father which is in heaven.

St. JAMES, the Apostle, CHAP. V.

2. But above all things, my Brethren, *Swear not*, neither by Heaven, neither by the Earth, neither by any other Oath; but let your Yea be yea, and your Nay, nay, lest ye fall into condemnation.

The Gospel, St. JOHN, CHAP. XII.

48. He that rejects me, *and receives not my words*, has one that judges him: the word that I have spoken *(which is the Gospel)*, the same shall judge him in the last day.

St. PAUL, Second Epistle to the THESSALONIANS, CHAP. I.

7. And to you who are troubled rest with us, when the Lord Jesus shall be revealed from heaven with his mighty angels;

8. In flaming fire, taking vengeance on them that know not God, and that obey not the Gospel of our Lord Jesus Christ.

As Circumcision to the Jews was the Seal of their covenant with GOD and promise of obedience to his Law, so is Baptism with Christians the Seal of their covenant with CHRIST and promise of obedience to his commands.

When Teachers professing Christianity have their maintenance and elevation in the World dependent on great, political, warlike Governments, and want to do from interested motives what the blessed Gospel prohibits, to add plausibility to their delusive reasons—as in the Legal and Religious case of Swearing Oaths, they go back to the Law of Moses for a precedent to justify their apostacy and conduct. The law was for the Jews alone, under the appointed administration of the Levites and Elders, in their own country; nevertheless, when strangers acknowledged God and submitted to its rights, they were also allowed the freedom of its benefit: but when Christ came into the world for the Redemption of Man, he abolished the Law, which was temporary, and in its place gave the Gospel, which is Everlasting. That is, he removed the form of worshipping God by sacrifice, the form of coming at the truth by swearing, and that of obtaining justice for injury by reprisal and violence.

—We

[43]

We all admire the Lord Jesus Christ for his humility and affection, the goodness and wisdom that breathes throughout his Gospel, and the sacrifice of himself for our Salvation; yet the generality of the world, as if unmindful of this wonderful instance of Divine love, not only refuse what they promised in Baptism to obey, but likewise seek by opposition and war to destroy his Salvation and happy Government of peace. What does a man require from his wife in marriage, but to love and be faithful to him only? Would he not be jealous and very angry if she obeyed any commands in opposition to his, and honoured another with the endearing name of husband? By the same rule, all that are baptized are by Covenant comparatively married to Christ; for the name of Christian implies a belief in him, and an obedience to his words. Is it wise or just then to obey a doctrine contrary to the commands of thy blessed Lord and acknowledged Saviour? And is it not unkind in thee, O Man, to honour thy equal with his sacred name?

As a man cannot in justice be considered as a Servant any longer than while he obeys the commands of his Master, so neither can a man in truth be regarded as a Christian any longer than while he obeys the commands of Christ.

Hear therefore, all nations, what the Lord commands me to write, and be warned by it, that as a Master is compelled to withdraw his allowance of food, and discharge from his house a Servant that will not obey him, so will he withdraw his loving kindness of Peace, and in anger remove from the face of the earth that Man or Family, City or Nation, that will only acknowledge Christ in word, but in practice refuse to obey his commands,

The XVIIth CHAP. of the REVELATION continued.

15. And he says to me, the waters which thou saw where the Whore sits, are People, and Multitudes, and Nations, and Tongues.

16. And the Ten Horns *(meaning the Cardinals)* which thou saw upon the Beast, *(meaning the Pope)* these shall hate the Whore, *(meaning Rome)* and shall make her desolate and naked, and shall eat her flesh and burn her with fire.

The Cardinals will disagree and quarrel, then Rome will be convulsed by Parties, and plundered alternately by each *(which means eating her Flesh);* in doing this, they will set the city on fire and almost destroy it. In due time after this, the latter part of the Nineteenth verse, in the Sixteenth Chapter, will be fulfilled on Rome, spiritually Babylon, the capital of Italy; when by a mighty Earthquake, the city with the ground it stands on will be lifted up, shook violently to pieces, and utterly overthrown.

17. For God has put in their hearts to fulfil his will, and to agree, and give their kingdom to the Beast, until the words of God shall be fulfilled.

The Cardinals will continue in subjection to the Pope, and agree in their measures of government, assisting him also with their Advice and Power, until the time already determined is expired, which is nearly so now; that done, the minds of the People will

be

be changed, and another spirit will be given to them, to fulfil the judgment of God according to this Prophecy.

I was not permitted to join this addition to this Book when first printed, which is the reason that it was passed over; but now I am commanded by the Lord my God, to print and join it to the former part, therefore I do.

RICHARD BROTHERS.

LONDON, 20th of the Month called SEPTEMBER, 1794.

A
REVEALED KNOWLEDGE,
OF THE
Prophecies & Times.

PARTICULARLY OF THE
PRESENT TIME, THE PRESENT WAR,
AND THE PROPHECY NOW FULFILLING.

THE YEAR OF THE WORLD 5913.

BOOK THE SECOND.

CONTAINING, WITH OTHER
GREAT AND REMARKABLE THINGS,
Not Revealed to any other Person on Earth,
THE SUDDEN AND PERPETUAL FALL OF THE
TURKISH, GERMAN, AND RUSSIAN
EMPIRES,

Wrote under the direction of the
LORD GOD,
AND PUBLISHED BY HIS SACRED COMMAND;
IT BEING A SECOND SIGN OF WARNING
FOR THE BENEFIT OF ALL NATIONS.

By the Man that will be Revealed to the HEBREWS
as their
PRINCE AND PROPHET.

LONDON.
PRINTED IN THE YEAR OF CHRIST

PREFACE.

LENGTH of time, change of countries and governments, corruption of language, and hasty copies in writing, before the more exact method of printing became generally used, has been the means of not only introducing, without design, into the Hebrew Bible, an insertion of some new words, but likewise an expulsion of some of the old, which produces a disagreement in some few parts, and makes it differ now from what it originally was in the times of David, Solomon, and at the commencement of the Babylonian captivity: some parts of the English translation are, consequently, erroneous; but they are so immaterial as not to affect, in the least, the truth of its sacred *Records*, or the tendency of its divine instruction.

The few parts of the English translation which I am instructed to alter in my writings, the propriety will be allowed by every person that has discernment to perceive, or conviction to believe:---beyond the limits of my authority, for it is prescribed, I am not suffered to proceed in any word or in any way whatever.

The following are the words which the Lord God spoke to me in a vision, soon after I was commanded to write and make known his judgments, for the good of London and general benefit of all nations:---There is no other man under the whole heaven that I discover the errors of the Bible to, and reveal a knowledge how to correct them, so that they may be restored as they were in the beginning, but yourself.

Moreover, when I began to write I believed it necessary to adopt the same language as the Scripture does, regularly imitating it in the words---ye, thee, and thou; but God spoke to me in a vision of the night, and said---Write in the same manner as I always speak to you; write as other men do; write according to the custom of the country you live in; you will then be better attended to, and what you write will be more easily understood.

PREFACE.

A man that has been an officer in the navy, whose immediate ancestors have been separated from the Jews such a considerable ~~length of time as to make them forget they ever~~ belonged to the name, such a man declaring himself openly to the world a prophet of God, the revealed Prince allotted to order the sudden return of the Hebrews from all nations, and govern them in the land of Israel, will, with some reason, I allow, excite both astonishment and doubt; but from the multiplied recorded testimonies I produce, which no other on earth can, it ought not to prevail with any person as a just objection against believing what I write.

For observe, some hostile profession was necessary for me to be engaged in, to fulfil the recorded judgment on the family I am designed to represent in the seat of government; therefore, with all the certain proofs I have and will constantly bring forward, with all the just reasons I advance, the surprize and doubt, entertained at the beginning, ought to vanish in as little time as would be requisite to read again the book which contains the account.

But remember likewise, from the records of Scripture, that Moses was taken away in his infancy, and remained separated from his brethren for eighty years; the first forty of which he was reared in the palace of the king of Egypt, and educated in the language and customs of the country like one of its own native princes; yet he was revealed to the Israelites as the prophet of God, to order their hasty departure from Pharoah's bondage, and afterwards to conduct them to the Promised Land.

Saul, the son of Kish, after being anointed king, prophecied in company with other men, to the great astonishment of all that saw him.

David, king of Isreal, the greatest favourite that ever God had on earth, whose wars, though many, originated at that time from necessity and justice, never undertook, but to prevent the introduction of idolatry, and preserve in the land of Israel a true uninterrupted worship of God, was a prophet; and for whose sake, in remembrance of his name, besieging armies were destroyed, and Jerusalem safely delivered. Yet this great monarch, this unequalled favourite, this pattern of mercy to all kings, and who alone, of all men under heaven, possessed the established promise of everlasting national government, could not, (but the objection did not proceed from any charge of injustice or sin,) for, being a man of war, and having shed much blood on the earth, although done by the express concurrence of the Most High, be permitted to build at Jerusalem a temple of worship for him: The great honour was given to Solomon, a king of peace, his son and immediate successor; so averse, though necessitated to order it, was the Creator of the world to the effusion of blood and the destruction of man.

PREFACE.

FIRST OF CHRONICLES.
CHAP. XXII.

7 And David said to Solomon, My son, as for me, it was in my mind to build a house to the name of the Lord my God.

8 But the word of the Lord came to me, saying, thou hast shed much blood, and hast made great wars; thou shalt not build a house to my name, because thou hast shed much blood on the earth in my sight.

9 Behold, a son shall be born to thee, who shall be a man of rest, and I will give him rest from all his enemies round about; for his name shall be Solomon, and I will give peace and quietness to Israel in his days.

10 He shall build a house for my name; and he shall be my son, and I will be his father; and I will establish his kingdom over Israel for ever.

SAMUEL was not only a priest, but likewise principal judge of Israel, yet he was a great prophet.

ISAIAH was a prince of the family of David, and likewise a prophet.

EZEKIEL was one of the principal priests.

JEREMIAH one of the poorer; yet both were alike great prophets.

AMOS was a poor herdsman of Tekoa, in the land of Israel;

DANIEL, a captive prince at Babylon, in Assyria; and yet both were great prophets.

GOD, without being accountable to any man for what he does, will sanctify, with his blessed Spirit, whom he pleases, however astonishing it may appear, and however incredible to the self righteous, that any person in preference to himself, should receive and be commanded to make known a communication of revealed knowledge;* but with God there is

---

* St. Paul was taught a knowledge of the Gospel by revelation, and instructed likewise how to preach it, before he could be an apostle, and joined to the ministry of Christ.

GALATIANS. CHAP. I.

11 But I certify to you, brethren, that the Gospel which was preached of me is not after man;

12 For I neither received it of man, neither was I taught it, but by the revelation of Jesus Christ.

no distinction of high or low, rich or poor; in his presence both are regarded alike, when just; and the Scripture abounds with many examples, recorded on purpose for after ages to imitate.

In the same manner that a knowledge of the Gospel, and how to preach it, was revealed to St. Paul, a knowledge of futurity, and those parts of the Scripture I have constantly mentioned, were revealed to me.

EPHESIANS. Chap. III.

2 If ye have heard of the dispensation of the grace of God, which is given me toward you:

3 How that by revelation he made known to me the mystery, as I wrote before in few words.

4 Whereby when ye read, ye may understand my knowledge in the mystery of Christ.

5 Which in other ages was not made known to the sons of men, as it is now revealed to his holy apostles and prophets by the spirit.

IN obedience to the sacred command of the Lord God, whose servant and prophet I am, I publish this writing, that it may be translated into all languages, for the information and benefit of all nations.

This is the last sign, and last warning, I am commanded to say, that will be given in writing before I am *revealed to the Jews*, when the commands delivered to me will be---to order them to depart in great haste from all nations, and go to the land of Israel: to repronounce the judgments of God, which have been suspended hitherto for my sake, and declare them irrevocable.

Of the PHROPHECY *which relates to the present time of the* WORLD, *the present* WAR, *and the approaching* DISTRESS *of all* NATIONS.

THE PROPHET DANIEL.
CHAP VII.

In the first year of Belshazzar, king of Babylon, Daniel had a dream, and visions in the night on his bed; then he wrote the visions, to shew the substance of what they contained.

2 Daniel spake and said; I saw in my vision by night, and behold, the four winds of the heaven strove on the great sea.

3 And *four great beasts* came up from the sea, different one from another.

4 The first was like a lion, and it had eagle's wings: I beheld 'till the wings were plucked, when it was lifted up on the earth, and made stand on the feet as a man; and a man's heart was given to it.

The lion means George the Third, the present king of England; plucking the wings of the lion, means taking away the power of the king; made stand on the feet as a man, with a man's heart, means his reduction to the condition of other men, and possessing similar thoughts.

It is more than twenty months since I first wrote to the king, queen, and minister of state, to inform them of many things that would come to pass; that the time was nearly accomplished, for some of the judgments of God to be made manifest, and also that this prophecy was fulfilling: I beseeched them in the most earnest and respectful language, not to join in the war on any account whatever, or even encourage it; for the death of Louis the Sixteenth would be impossible to prevent, it was recorded, and could not be avoided; the revolution in France, and its consequences, proceeded entirely from the judgment of God to fulfil the prophecy of Daniel: therefore all attempts to overthrow the judgment, and preserve the monarchy by force, was opposing what was determined in the Scripture of Truth should most certainly take place.

The aspect of the war was delusive, the encouragements of success that it held out to princes were deceitful; but those encouragements of delusion were permitted, to bring many nations under the judgment of God, and punish them for the heavy guilt of opposing his decrees.

If many had no more to fight against than a few men alone, or nations but one divided nation to subdue, then it might with reason be expected that the greatest number would soon overcome the least, and that many strong nations would soon conquer a weak one: but it is many men fighting against the Spirit of God, and strong nations labouring in vain with their blood and treasure to overthrow his Judgment.

The Lord God permits this opposition for three years and a half, to fulfil the determined part of this prophecy on all that oppose it; that done, his judgments will take place, to punish man and lay waste kingdoms.

St. John the Apostle, in the nineteenth chapter of the Revelation, alludes to the present time of the world, and means the same things, though differently described, as the prophet Daniel does in the seventh chapter; for which I am commanded to insert a part, that all princes and governments may be publicly warned, that they may know the consequences of this war, from the judgment of God, will be---death to millions, and everlasting distress to all nations.

10 And I fell at his feet to worship him, and he said to me, see thou do it not; I am thy fellow-servant, and of thy brethren that have the testimony of Jesus; worship God: for the testimony of Jesus is the spirit of prophecy.

11 And I saw heaven opened; and behold a white horse; and he that sat on him was called Faithful and True: and in righteousness he doth judge and make war.

12 His eyes were as a flame of fire, and on his head were many crowns; and he had a name written that no man knew but he himself.

13 And he was cloathed with a vesture dipped in blood: and his name is called, The Word of God.

14 And the armies which were in heaven followed him on white horses, cloathed in fine linen, white and clean.

The armies are an allusion to the powerful judgments of God, under what---or how many different forms their visitation of death is made on the world.

15 And out of his mouth goes a sharp sword, that with it he should smite the nations: and he will rule them with a rod of iron; and he treads the wine-press of the fierceness and wrath of Almighty God.

16 And he has on his vesture and on his thigh a name written, King of kings, and Lord of lords.

17 And I saw an angel standing in the sun; and he cried with a loud voice, (meaning thunder, which is explained in the first book of Revealed Knowledge) saying to all the fowls that fly in the midst of heaven, come and gather yourselves together to the supper of the great God.

18 That ye may eat the flesh of kings, and the flesh of captains, and the flesh of mighty men, and the flesh of horses, and of them that sit on them; and the flesh of all men, both free and bond, both small and great.

19 And I saw the beast, and the kings of the earth, and their armies gathered together, to make war against him that sat on the horse, and against his army.

20 And the beast was taken, and with him the false prophet that wrought miracles before him, with which he deceived them that had received the mark of the beast, and them that worshipped his image. These both were cast alive into a lake of fire burning with brimstone.

21 And the remnant were slain with the sword of him that sat on the horse, which sword proceeded out of his mouth; and all the fowls were filled with their flesh.

DANIEL, CHAP. VII. CONTINUED.

5 And, behold, another beast; a second, like a bear: and it raised itself up on one side, with three ribs in its mouth between its teeth; and they said thus to it, Arise, devour much flesh.

This verse means the present Empress of Russia: She is according to the judgment of God in this prophecy, decreed to suffer death: and by revelation I am informed it will be done by the hands of man.

6 After this I beheld, and lo, another like a leopard: which had on its back four wings of a fowl; the beast had also four heads, and dominion was given to it.

The Leopard, means Louis the Sixteenth king of France: the wings of a fowl on its back, is, like the eagle's on the lion, an allusion to the king's great moveable power.

The fall of this monarch from a throne, and afterwards suffering death, to fulfil the judgment of God by his prophet Daniel, was impossible for all the armies of Europe to prevent; equally so as the decreed death of Charles the First, king of England, which is mentioned by St. John in the thirteenth chapter and third verse of the Revelation; *the deadly wound being healed*, in the same verse means the *recovery* of monarchy *by the restoration* of Charles the Second.

7 After this I saw in the night visions a fourth beast; and behold, it, was dreadful, and terrible and strong exceedingly; and it had great iron teeth: it devoured, broke in pieces, and stamped on the residue (meaning the electors) with its feet; it was different from all the beasts that were seen before, and it had ten horns.

This great beast, so different from the others, means the pre-

B

sent emperor of Germany; the ten horns, mean the electors, or princes of the empire.

In one part of this chapter the horns are denominated kings; the reason is, they raise armies, go to war and govern with absolute power, like them; but notwithstanding, they all accknowledge the emperor as their chief, and under that acknowledgment of subjection are solemnly engaged to defend his empire when called on. For which, to conceal the meaning of the prophecy, until the fullness of time comes and the appointed person for it to be revealed to, the vision represents the German princes as horns of defence belonging to the emperor's head.

It devoured, broke in pieces, and stamped on the residue with its feet—means the entire destruction of the German electors; and the possession of their territories by the emperor: he will destroy them, and also spread his dominion over Italy; threatening at the same time all Europe, and despising its kings with their feeble efforts to oppose him, Rome will fall under his power and so will Venice likewise; the former will be retaken by the French republic, but the latter will be plundered and almost destroyed. After this, to fulfil the prophecy and the judgment of God, he will suffer death from the hands of man.

The orders of the emperor, in the Netherlands, are, that if the Austrian army should be defeated, *and it most surely will*; for I am commanded to repeat as an example and warning, what the prophet Jeremiah was commanded to say to the messengers of Zedekiah, king of Judah:

CHAP. XXXVII.

9 Thus says the Lord; Deceive not yourselves, saying, The Chaldeans will surely depart from us: for they shall not depart.

10 For though he has smitten the whole army of the Chaldeans that fight against you, and there remained but wounded men, yet they should rise up, every man in his tent, and burn this city with fire.

By the same example, if the French army was to be defeated, even again and again, it should recover and conquer likewise; (that all the judgments of God, in the seventh chapter of the prophecy of Daniel, may take their course, and be fulfilled,) to acknowledge the French republic, and make an immediate peace on the best terms that can be obtained, the interests of other nations will not be much consulted; time the threats of a victorious enemy, and the perilous condition of the German army, will not admit the least delay.

The English will sharply remonstrate against this conduct; for which their army, however incredible it may appear to the Government now, will be surrounded, disarmed, and commanded to depart: but their general will be detained by the Austrian; and, by revelation from the Lord God to me, he falls to the ground.

The emperor, being exhausted of money by the war, but having a large army at his command, determines, now he has made peace with the French, and quarrelled with the English, to execute the plan he has for some time conceived the hopes of being one day able to accomplish---his father and uncle, strange as it may appear, yet it is most certainly true, for I am informed, by revelation, conceived the same design, and believed the attempt easily practicable when the opportunity offered, which is---*the reduction of all Germany, under the sole government of himself.*

He begins with seizing on the electorate of Hanover, and plundering it quite bare : after this success, his ambition for more extensive dominion will rise ; it will now lead him boldly forward to subject and devour them all. For God, to fulfil his judgments, and this prophecy of Daniel, in chaper vii. will deliver him over, to be governed by the secret, but powerful workings of an evil spirit ; because his inclinations are bad : according to all that I informed the king and queen of, in May and June 1792 ; as he did Ahab, king of Israel, to accomplish his fall, and the entire destruction of his family.

FIRST OF KINGS.

CHAP. XXII.

4 And he said to Jehoshaphat, Wilt thou go with me to the battle to Ramoth Gilead ? And Jehoshaphat said to the king of Israel, I am the same as thou, my people as thy people, my horses as thy horses.

5 And Jehoshaphat said to the king of Israel, Enquire, I pray thee, from the word of the Lord to-day.

6 Then the king of Israel gathered the prophets together, about four hundred men, and said to them, Shall I go against Ramoth Gilead to battle, or shall I forbear ? and they said, Go up ; for the Lord will deliver it into the hand of the king.

7 And Jehoshaphat said, Is there not here a prophet of the Lord besides, that we might enquire of him ?

8 And the king of Israel said to Jehoshaphat, There is one man yet, Micaiah, the son of Imlah, by whom we may enquire of the Lord : but I hate him, for he does not prophecy good of me, but evil. And Jehoshaphat said, Let not the king say so.

11 And Zedekiah, the son of Chenaanah, made horns of iron ; and he said, Thus says the Lord, with these thou sha'lt push the Syrians, until thou consume them.

12 And all the prophets prophecied so, saying, Go up to Ramoth Gilead, and prosper : for the Lord will deliver it into the king's hand.

13 And the messenger that was gone to call Micaiah, spake to him, saying, Behold now, the words of the prophets are as one mouth, declaring good to the king : let thy word, I pray thee, be like the word of one of them, and speak that

14 And Micaiah said, As the Lord lives, what the Lord says to me, that will I speak:

17 And he said, I saw all Israel scattered on the hills, as sheep which have not a shepherd: and the Lord said, These have no master; let them return, every man to his house in peace.

18 And the king of Israel said to Jehoshaphat, Did I not tell thee, that he would prophecy no good for me, but evil?

19 And he said, Hear thou therefore the word of the Lord: I saw the Lord sitting on his throne, and all the host of heaven standing by him, on his right hand and on his left.

20 And the Lord said, Who will persuade Ahab, that he may go up and fall at Ramoth Gilead; and one said in this manner, and another said in that manner.

21 And there came forth a Spirit, and he stood before the Lord, and said, I will persuade him.

22 And the Lord said to him, In what manner? And he said, I will go forth, and I will be a lying spirit in the mouth of all his prophets. And he said, Thou shalt persuade him, and prevail also: Go forth, and do so.

23 Now, therefore, behold, the Lord God has put a lying spirit in the mouth of all these thy prophets, and the Lord has spoken of evil concerning thee.

The Emperor's council will be filled with the same delusive evil spirit, that they may concur with him, and possess the same violent inclination for war and human destruction as himself. At this time a fresh decree will be issued from Vienna, commanding all Germany, and all the people under his government, as he conquers them by fire and sword, to offer solemn prayers up to the Lord God, for the further success of his imperial Majesty's arms, the entire destruction of his enemies, and the preservation of himself; styling him, *in blasphemy against God*, their most Gracious, Just, and Merciful Sovereign Lord.

The other nations of Europe, afraid and trembling, will as solemnly implore the same Lord God for peace and safety, against such a cruel enemy, forgetting, that it was but a little time before, they were praying in the same strain of blasphemy as himself---*To destroy their enemies, and give success to their arms;* to that very gracious and compassionate God, who sealed the redemption of man with his own blood, and strictly commanded all nations, as his children and people, to live in peace and brotherly love.

Opposition is in vain: he goes through the principalities like lations he destroyed, whose towns he plundesed and burnt but a little time before. This is Francis, the present reigning emperor of Germany, who is described, in chap. vii. ver. 7. of the prophecy of Daniel, as great, strong, and terrible; stamping under his feet with contempt, and destroying all the princes round him. His ambition will increase with his dominion, and his conquests will be so wonderful, for a short time, as to make all Europe tremble; his end is miserable; and as he treated others without mercy, no mercy will be shewn to him. His death, by the hands of man is certain, because decreed; and his punishment everlasting, because recorded. To be related to him now, will be considered hereafter as a capital crime.

DANIEL, CHAP. VII. CONTINUED.

8 I considered the horns, and behold there came up among them another little horn, before whom there were three of the first horns plucked up by the roots; and behold, in this horn were eyes like the eyes of man, and a mouth speaking great things.

This little horn, that grows great, and becomes so ambitious as to pluck up three of the other horns, to extend his own dominion, is the present King of Prussia. He is one of the imperial electors, and to fulfil exactly what the visions of God describe him to be, he confidently calls himself, in great words, The preponderating member of the Germanic body.

The king of Prussia will acknowledge the French republic, and also make peace with it: he will oppose the Emperor, and likewise follow his example; by which his dominions, to fulfil the prophecy, will be enlarged (comparitively for a moment only) by the addition of three electorates, when the Bear, (meaning Russia,) watching for the opportunity, *will rise* and devour Prussia at one side, while the Emperor destroys him at the other. His armies will be defeated, and his capital set on fire by the Bear: his life will be taken away from the earth, and his monarchy, to fulfil the everlasting decrees of the Lord God, in the prophecy of Daniel, will be destroyed; never, never, to be restored any more.

Russia will assist the Emperor in the beginning, to promote her favourite design of destroying the Turkish empire; she will also quarrel with the Poles, and devour great numbers of them; Warsaw will be set on fire, and the government entirely changed. At this time the Russian army, (or Bear,) as if impatient for its food, *to rise and devour much flesh*, will enter Turkey, and comparatively run over the land; treading down, and devouring with great fury, all opposition in its way. At the capital it stops; here are its decreed bounds; no farther it must go. Here the Russian general divides the spoils of many cities with his army, and the rich provinces of Turkey between his officers. Here he despises the oath of fidelity, and throws away the submission of a subject—pro-

After this the Swede will enter Russia, and destroy with great fury; even the ships of war and capital will not escape. The Russian empire will be convulsed in many parts by its generals and governors, each rising up in his place, and claiming an authority to command the other; they will fight until great multitudes are destroyed, and the country made desolate. The imperial family will all be cut off, and no successor will for ever after arise; the Government, at the same time, will be broke to pieces, and utterly dissolved; never, never, to be restored any more.

The Spanish Monarchy will cease by this war, and the Stadtholdership of Holland will be cut off close to the ground; according to the visions of God to me, in 1792, and which I communicated at that time by his sacred command to the king and queen of England.

The king of Sardinia will be dethroned, and the Popedom destroyed for ever! according to the revelation of God to me, and which I communicated to the English prime minister before the war with France was entered into; concluding what I wrote to him with these words---It is not all the navy of England, nor the armies of Europe united, can prevent the king of Sardinia from being dethroned.

The *death of the French king*, as one of the particular number, mentioned in the seventh chapter of Daniel, decreed to die, took place, to fulfil the predetermined judgment of God by this prophet; the monarchy of France is likewise, by the same judgment, abolished for ever, and the present form of government established. Therefore marvel no more that it cannot be conquered by all the armies without, nor destroyed by all the commotions within; if it could, by human power, the *Horn* (meaning the king of Prussia) would be the allotted man to accomplish it: for the meaning of the prophecy is, that he shall prevail against France for three years and a half, but not to conquer the whole: he would have faithfully kept with his army in France the promises he made with his mouth on entering it; which were, to deliver over the towns for plunder, and the people for death, if he was opposed. It is for this that he is described by Daniel, to have a *mouth speaking great things and blasphemies*. All this would have been permitted, because recorded, to fulfil the prophecy; to hasten his own destruction, and the general fall of *European Monarchy*.

The Dutch will acknowledge the French republic, and also make a hasty peace with it; the Portuguese will do the same.

TO THE KING AND PARLIAMENT
OF
GREAT BRITAIN.

HEAR what the Lord God additionally says to me by revelation, and commands me to write—*France* seeing England ditions of peace, an acknowledgment of the republic, a restoration of the colonies, and the ships taken away from Toulon. For a short time he will permit *England*, as he will *Russia* and *Germany*, to succeed in the acquisition of delusive conquest, but it is the better---the more effectual, and more imperceptible to human foresight, to accomplish his judgment on her, according to the prophecy of Daniel and Revelation of St. John; after that short time is expired, which is nearly so now, new enemies will rise up, some warring against her openly, others privately; all will prevail, until she that sits now, as a *queen among the nations*, is, according to the vision of God, in my first book, without a covering on her head, worn thread-bare, and rent in many places.

Will England continue this war any longer against a people that has the judgment of God in their favour? Will she, by a continuance of the present war against France, enter into another, for the safety of Hanover, against the Emperor of Germany, who will be rendered invincible for a time, as a *scourge*, to fulfil the recorded judgments of God? Will she continue this war any longer for her destruction, that she may enter into a fresh one with America to hasten it? Is the king of England so regardless of his own life, and the preservation of his family, as to involve them with himself in certain misery and death, by a longer continuance of this war? Is the government, the parliament, the clergy and people, so insensible to the blessings of peace, and the happiness of fortune, as to prefer the absolute certainty of losing all they possess, and being destroyed themselves, to support a war which, in its consequences, to fulfil the judgment of God, is designed shall throw down, for ever, the English monarchy; and from the confusion it will make, throughout the country, involve almost every family of wealth in beggary and death?

Are you, William Pitt, to whom I wrote in May and June 1792, informing you of the consequences of this war to your country, when the war was not intended, so insensible to your own preservation and the benefit of your brother, as to continue any longer a war that will involve both you and him in certain death? What I acquainted you with in 1792, and often since, was made known to me by *visions and revelations* from the Lord God. The *death of Louis* XVI. and the removal of the English crown from the king's head, to a level with the ground, according to the seventh chapter of Daniel; the fall of the queen's palace, and the destruction of the Tower; your own removal from administration, and afterwards death, was among the things which I informed you of would most certainly come to pass as the evil consequences of this delusive war. My account to you then, of futurity, concluded with these words---
" The visions are established, and the things mentioned most certain and true."

When I informed you that England would enter into this war, and the consequences which would, in despite of all your efforts, flow from it; *you despised me;* for, at that time, the war was not intended, and to tell of evils that would most certainly ensue from a thing, when the thing they were to proceed from was not designed, were to you the effects of folly and deceit.

My knowledge of future things is given me from God; therefore what I wrote was true: A little time longer, and England will be so much entangled as not to be able to go forward without feeling the pains of that *colonial conquest* which is to be the cause of her death; nor to retire, without falling under that foreign blow, which will break the empires in pieces, and throw herself down on the ground; from whence she is never to rise up any more.

Neither evil can be prevented, and both will take place, to fulfil the *judgment of God*, according to the prophecy of Daniel and Revelation of St. John; *unless what I write is believed to be true, and the advice I give is strictly followed.* Fleets and armies are great things to talk of, because terrible to destroy mankind; but, when opposed by the power of heaven, they become weak, they lose their force and terror; for most of those in Europe are destined for the rocks and the flames: They are permitted to conquer a little for a short time now; but it is, like Russia and Germany, to hasten that dreadful fall of human government which will soon take place in the world: for they ever have been, in the hand of God, the very instruments to effect what princes designed to prevent.

On the 12th of the month called May 1792, I wrote to the king, minister of state, and speaker of the commons, that no person should be able to say, hereafter, my conduct was irregular, or in the least disrespectful, to inform them that I was commanded, by the Lord God, to go to the Parliament-house on the 17th following, and acquaint the members, for their own personal safety, and the general benefit of the country---That the time of the world was come to fulfil the seventh chapter of the prophecy of Daniel, and some of the judgments of God in the Revelation; that the death of Louis XVI. and the revolution in France, for the perpetual destruction of its monarchy, was decreed in the Scripture of truth; and would, against all human opposition, most surely take place: To inform them that the war, just going to be commenced, by Prussia and Austria, against France, was the very war alluded to by St. John, in the Revelation, chap xix. which God called a war against himself; because it went to oppose his decrees, and because it would be an effort of kings to overthrow his unalterable judgment. I was commanded to advise them, as I was the *king* and *minister of state*, not to join in the war, or even encourage it on any account whatever: To inform them of the approaching fall of monarchy in Europe, the great distress this war would be productive of to all nations, but particularly to those that engaged in it: and likewise to inform them of their own sudden fall in the jaws of the earth by a pre-determined earthquake, according to the judgment of God, in chap. xvi. ver. 16, 17, 18 and 19, of the Revelation; and, lastly, to entreat them to acknowledge this gracious communication from God, for their length of life and blessing, by an obedience to his good advice.

When at the door, on the 17th, I informed the Speaker by a letter, that I waited, and was ready to communicate all that I was commanded. In a few minutes after a messenger returned, with my own letter, who treated me, *in such a public place particularly*, with unfeeling contempt and incivility. The Lord God spoke to me instantly, on being ordered to go about my business, and said—Get away, get away from this place; be under no concern, it was not you that was despised and ordered away, but me, in your person, that sent you.

Soon after my return home I was in a *vision*, and saw a large measuring rod move through the streets in great haste, and strike many of the houses as it passed, marking them for their approaching fall. After this I was made to look towards the *Treasury*, while the Lord God pronounced, at the same time— *All that side shall fall*. In an instant, the whole place was covered with thick darkness; it seemed to be everlasting darkness; darkness that should never be removed: And, again, he pronounced, in quick words, as if displeased—The whole shall fall.

The information, as will be plainly seen by the date, which I gave to the *king* and *minister of state*, with what I was commanded to offer to the parliament, was not only before the present war with France was entered into, but also some length of time before it was ever intended: therefore no person can say, with justice, that either my conduct in obeying the positive commands of God, or my endeavours to preserve peace; to preserve this country from the many evils it has now to encounter with, according to the determined judgment of unerring prophecy; originated from weak ideas or political motives. No, my knowledge is given from God; I see all things now as they truly are; and know their consequences, to change them to what they really will be hereafter.

I am commanded to keep no company, and live retired; that I may avoid the temptation of political discussion, or any other argument, that would create animosity and strife.

The Two Parts of the REVELATION, *to be fulfilled on* LONDON, *and the* ENGLISH PRALIAMENT, *according to the Judgment of God; but are immediately suspended for my Entreaty.*

CHAP. XI.

3 AND I will give power to my two witnesses, and they shall prophecy a thousand two hundred and threescore days,

The *two witnesses*, the *two olive trees*, and the *two candlesticks*, mean the same two parts of the *everlasting Gospel of Salvation*, as they are wrote by St. Matthew and St. John; which are the two *apostles* and *proper* witnesses of Christ.

This explanation alone, which has never been discovered to any before, is sufficient to strike every man with conviction, that studies the Scripture, and believes in the spirit of God, that, as this part is true, the others I have, and shall constantly mention, are equally so; and that a knowledge of the whole comes directly to me from the Divine Being.

As the eyes of the blind cannot be opened, nor the sick healed, but by the immediate power of God; so neither can the prophecies be truly explained, but by regular instruction from the same *Almighty Being*.

Read diligently what follows, and by the information contemplate on the mighty goodness of God, for revealing a true knowledge of his prophecies in sufficient time to implore for mercy, and save a *city*, with *multitudes of people*, recorded to be destroyed.

7 And when they shall have finished their testimony, the beast that ascends out of the bottomless pit will make war against them, and will overcome them, and kill them.

8 And their dead bodies shall lie in the street of the great city, which is spiritually called Sodom in Egypt, where also our Lord was crucified.

This great city mentioned here, means *London*: her streets are full of prostitutes, and many of her houses are full of *crimes*. It is for such exceeding great wickedness, that St. John *spiritually* calls *London*, in this chapter, by the name of *Sodom*, and infers, from the toleration of so much evil, that the two witnesses of Christ, that the two apostles, St. Matthew and St. John, spiritually represented by the two parts of the Gospel, which they wrote, that their two bodies lie dead---thrown out in the street---trampled under the foot of vice.

11 And after three days and a half the spirit of life from God entered into them, and they stood upon their feet, and great fear fell on all that saw them.

The three days and a half, *means three years and a half*; and the present is the time of the world alluded to by St. John: for until the present war, of *time, times*, and the *dividing of time*, which is three years and a half, according to the 7th chapter of Daniel, also is expired, the two parts of the blessed Gospel will lie dead in London, and over Europe likewise: after which, a and throw it on the ground, when it will be changed into a serpent; to take it in my hand again, when it will be re-changed a rod.) The people of London will then tremble, and all nations will be greatly afraid, when they hear the dreadful consequences for neglecting them so long.

12 And they heard a great voice from heaven, (meaning thunder) saying to them, Come up hither. And they ascended up to heaven in a cloud, and their enemies beheld them.

13 And the same hour there was a great earthquake, and the tenth part of the city fell; and in the earthquake were slain of men seven thousand, and the remainder were affrighted, and gave glory (meaning honour) to the God of heaven.

The recorded judgment of God, according to this last verse, is, that London, for indeed it is the city meant, shall be visited by an earthquake, and a tenth part of it destroyed; in that tenth part, about seven thousand persons will be killed. When the people see this, they will be convinced that it proceeds from the great anger of God, for despising his offered mercy, and treating his messenger ill; then they will all be frightened, and will all believe: Then the city will honour him by instant reformation, and all the people will implore him for pity.

Lot was laughed at, and the danger despised by his sons in-law, when he said to them, " Up, get you out of this place, for the Lord will destroy this city." Sodom was burnt, and they perished.

The king of Nineva'h, although a professed idolater, and immersed in wickedness, believed the judgment of God by his prophet when he heard it, *without the additional testimony of scriptural evidence*; he immediately humbled himself, reformed, and entreated for mercy; by doing so, the city was forgiven, and all its people saved.

14 The second woe is past, and behold the third woe comes quickly.

CHAP. XVI.

This part which follows belongs to the thirteenth chapter; and is a continuation of the account begun there of the rise, progress, and perpetual fall of the English government.

13 And I saw three unclean spirits like frogs come out of the mouth of the dragon, and out of the mouth of the beast, and out of the mouth of the false prophet.

14 For they are the spirits of devils, working miracles, which

that sin is always committed by man through the temptation of Satan, (for there is no man on earth that does not do wrong at times, neither is there any that is not a sinner; look at the words of Solomon in his prayer when the Temple was dedicated.) This proclamation then being blasphemous, is in the same manner directed by his secret and powerful influence.

16 And he (meaning the king) gathered them together into a place, called in the Hebrew tongue Armageddon.

Them, means the *Parliament;* *Armageddon,* their house to assemble and die in.

Armageddon was a valley to bury the dead in, and also a place of great mourning, near Jerusalem: the Parliament House in London being the *recorded prophecied* burying-place of its members, and multitudes besides, is, for its designed similiarity to the former, spiritually called in the Hebrew tongue by the same name.

17 And the seventh angel poured out his vial in the air; and there came a great voice (meaning loud thunder) out of the Temple of heaven, from the Throne, saying—" IT IS DONE."

This verse means, that when the allotted time is expired for the English parliament to exist, the Lord God will pronounce from the Throne of heaven, in a voice of very loud thunder, the judgment of its utter destruction on a sudden.

18 And there were voices, and thunders, and lightnings; and there was a great earthquake, such as was not since men were upon the earth, so mighty an earthquake and so great.

The judgment of God being to destroy the English Parliament, this mighty earthquake will swallow it up at the very time of its sitting; and likewise so much of London, as to leave but three divisions of it standing.

19 And the great city was divided into three parts; and the cities of the nations fell: and great Babylon (meaning Rome in this chapter) came in remembrance before God, to give to her the cup of the wine of the fierceness of his wrath.

20 And every island fled away, and the mountains were not found.

The city mentioned here, under the name of the great city, means London; this *designed recorded earthquake* will be felt in all nations under heaven as well as in England, and its dreadful effects by most cities in the world as well as London. The earth will be shook so violently at this time as to make it sink in many places, and let the sea flow in where the land was: mountains will sink to a level with vallies, and many islands will disappear for ever in the sea. This earthquake will spread desolation throughout all countries, and destroy great multitudes of people.

The United States of America will declare war against England; but before they do, *France* will lose all her West India Islands; and after they do, Jamaica will be the last in the pos-

On the 25th of June, 1792, I wrote to the French ambassador then in London, by command of the Lord God, acquainting him with the future loss of the French Islands, and likewise the fall of the English. But he treated it in the same manner as all the writings of the prophets of God ever have been, when they sent divine information, when they spoke the truth, when they did not flatter with pleasing words to deceive.

There will great changes take place in all nations under heaven, to fulfil this prophecy of Daniel by visions in the seventh chapter: Nation will not only rise against nation, but they will be likewise torn by civil wars in themselves; kingdom will rise against kingdom, and man against man; until they fight and fall—to rise no more, The sword will destroy very great multitudes of people by this war, and occasion frightful desolations over the earth.

The promise of God by the prophet Haggai to Zerubbabel, Governor of Judah, although mentioned in the first book, I am commanded to repeat it here, means the present time of the world, and the present war with its destructive consequences; and myself the man, in whom this great promise of wonderful distinction and elevation is to be fulfilled.

CHAP. II

20 AND again the word of the Lord came to Haggai in the four and twentieth day of the month saying—

21 Speak to Zerubbabel, governor of Judah, and say, I will shake the heavens and the earth.

22 And I will overthrow the thrones of kingdoms, and I will destroy the strength of the kingdoms of the heathen; I will overthrow their chariots, and those that ride in them; their horses and riders shall come down, every one by the sword of the other.

The present time of the world, and this present war in its spreading consequences, is the time of trouble and destruction meant by the prophet: this is also the Great War recorded by Daniel and St. John, that no man has a knowledge of its progress and how it will end revealed to him but myself: this is the war which will fill up the measure of transgression, and carry the guilt of shedding innocent blood into all nations: the sword is drawn in heaven, and the cup of fury held out to the earth, according to the prophecies in the scripture, and the visions of God shewn to me, which are recorded by his sacred command in the first book; therefore she must drink deep from the one, that she may feel less the bitterness of death from the other, until wasted of her inhabitants.

23 In that day, says the Lord of Hosts, I will take thee, O Zerubbabel, my servant, the son of Shelathiel, and will make thee as a signet; for I have chosen thee, says the Lord of Hosts.

The promise of God to Zerubbabel, by the prophet Haggai,

dant; who will be not only like himself, the visible prince and governor for the Jews, but also receive the full performance of this great promise; which is, to be regarded by all nations as their signet of peace and safety.

The covenant to king David, and the renewal of it to Solomon, with this recorded promise to Zerubbabel, will be fulfilled in me; for which the Lord God, through this writing, holds me out now as the promised signet in his hand to all nations that believe in him, and commands me to say, That his recorded judgments, in the Scripture, according to all that I have mentioned, according to the prophecies of Daniel, Haggai, and St. John in the Revelation, for the *fall* of cities, the *fall* of thrones, the *fall* of princes, the *death* of millions, and the *desolation* of kingdoms, shall be suspended again, if the nations at war will accept of life, and return to his government of peace.

But if they allow themselves to be led away by delusive temptations, if they refuse to believe that I am commanded to offer these things, although supported by undeniable proofs of Scripture, of revealed knowledge in this book, as well as in the first, which are unkown to any other, and which were never made known to any man, before: if they will not accept of this gracious offer of mercy for their length of life now, and the good of their children hereafter, all I have mentioned, all the prophecies of Daniel, Haggai, and St. John in the Revelation, which relate to the present time of the world and the present war, will be fulfilled:—the sword must go through, and earthquakes will soon follow; *thrones* will be destroyed, *cities* levelled with the ground, *millions* of *people* will be cut off, and *kingdoms* will be made desolate for ever.

The Lord God, the better to make all nations believe immediately, and the people I live among regard me as his prophet, for their benefit in future, gave me the true age of the world, by which he fulfils his recorded judgments, and taught me, by direct instruction from himself, how to write it down; the time of shewing his mercy to the Jews, by their restoration; the true meaning of the prophecies, and time of fulfilling them, with his commands to publish the information to the world; that when I am openly revealed to the Hebrews and people of London, *(to the former,* to order their immediate departure from England, under my own direction; *to the latter,* to convince them, the loud thunder, in January 1791, was to proclaim the judgment of God and fall of London; *but that the judgment was suspended and the city pardoned, for my entreaty,)* and ordered to re-pronounce, with the power of fire, his irrevocable judgments, no nation may be able to say, We were not informed of any offers of mercy from God, or of those things which would lead us to believe the age of the world, was so great, and the prophecies of desolation were fulfilling; for the king and principal members of the *English government,* with nearly all the foreign *ambassadors* in London for their respective countries, have

THE PROPHECY OF DANIEL,

In the Seventh Chapter, continued.

9 I BEHELD till the thrones were cast down, and the Ancient of Days did sit; whose garment was white as snow, and the hair of his head like pure wool; his throne was like the fiery flame, and his wheels as burning fire.

This verse alone, unassisted by any information from me, is sufficient to explain the most necessary parts of the chapter to know; every person that reads it must confess that it alludes to the latter time of the world, and that the general dissolution of human grandeur, which it mentions, is but the expected necessary preparation for the coming of Christ, to judge the world.

10. A fiery stream issued, and came forth from before him; thousand thousands ministered to him, and ten thousand times ten thousand stood before him: the judgment was set, and the books were opened.

The latter part of this verse corroborates the explanation that is given of the preceding one.

11 I beheld then, because the voice of the great words which the horn spoke—is *the king of Prussia*—(here the prophet Daniel returns to the former part of the vision, and gives a further account of what was shewn him.) I beheld, even till the beast was slain, and his body destroyed, and given to the burning flame.

The death of this *beast*, means the death of the emperor of Germany, it is certain; and all the armies of Europe cannot save him, nor prevent the accomplishment of it by the hands of man. The judgment of God, according to this prophecy, is also, that he shall suffer the punishment of everlasting fire.

12 As concerning the rest of the beasts, they had their dominion taken away; yet their lives were prolonged for a season and time.

13 I saw in the night visions, one like the Son of man; and behold, he came with the clouds of heaven, and came to the Ancient of Days, and stood near before him.

14 And there was given him dominion, and glory, and a kingdom; that all people, nations, and languages,

should serve him : his dominion is an everlasting dominion, which shall not pass away ; and his kingdom that which shall not be destroyed.

15 I, Daniel, was grieved in my spirit in the midst of my body, and the visions I saw troubled me.

16 I came near to one of them that stood by, (*an angel*,) and asked him the meaning of all these things; so he told me, and made me understand the interpretation of them.

The prophet Daniel, in his visions, as well as St. John the apostle in the Revelation, had always an attending angel near, to explain the meaning of every thing he saw that was necessary for him to be informed of.

17 These great beasts, which are four, are four kings, which shall arise out of the earth.

18 But the saints of the Most High shall take the kingdom, and possess the kingdom for ever, even for ever and ever.

The time is very nearly come for the *judgments of God to be felt in all nations*, and this part of the prophecy to be fulfilled in Europe : It is a warning to all princes and states, to honour God, and fear his judgments ; to live in peace, and govern with mercy.

19 Then I asked him the meaning of the fourth beast, which was different from all the others, and exceeding dreadful ! whose teeth were of iron, and its nails of brass ; which devoured, broke in pieces, and stamped on the residue with its feet.

20 And of the ten horns that were in its head, and of the other which came up, before whom three fell ; even of that horn which had eyes, and a mouth that spake very great things, whose look was more stout than his fellows.

The beginning of this verse means the German Princes ; the rest of it the King of Prussia ; he threatens and executes more; presuming on the unconquerable power of his army, than any of his equals. His being represented in the visions of God as a horn, with eyes, and a mouth speaking very great things, is an allusion to his military strength, quick discernment, and violent inclination to quarrel; always disputing for territory, pushing at or fighting against some nation or other.

21 I beheld, and the same horn made war on the saints,

For my entreaty, the Lord God has been pleased to suspend this part of the prophecy, the latter part of the twenty-first verse, that of allowing the King of Prussia to prevail against the righteous, and govern them with great oppression, under the power of his army, for three years and a half.

22 Until the Ancient of Days came, when judgment was given for the saints of the Most High, and the time came that the saints should possess the kingdom.

23 Thus he said; The fourth beast will be the fourth kingdom on earth. (The Emperor will reduce, under his subjection, all Germany, the neighbouring states, and all Italy, to form this great kingdom) which will be different from all the other kingdoms; (meaning the other great kingdoms or monarchies, shewn in the visions; which are, England, Russia, and France.) It will try to devour the whole earth, tread it down, and break it in pieces.

24. And the ten horns, out of his kingdom (meaning the German electors, before they are destroyed by the Emperor) are ten kings which will arise; and another will arise after them (meaning the king of Prussia, who is an elector; he will be different from the first, and will subdue three kings.

When the King of Prussia opposes the Emperor, he will also at the same time follow his example, which will soon now begin to manifest itself; indeed, the interval of time between this and then is but short; for all things are hastening fast, and concurring in their operations, to extend the war, and give the prophecy its full recorded course.

25 And he will speak great words against the Most High, and will wear out the saints of the Most High; and will think to change times and laws: and they will be given into his hand, for a time, and times, and the dividing of time.

The beginning of this verse means the King of Prussia, speaking in *blasphemy* against God, threatening in great words, as if he possessed the whole power of heaven, to conquer and destroy, with his army, all cities that do not open to him, and all men that oppose his designs. This was exactly fulfilled by the Horn, when he entered France in 1792; the proclamations which he issued at that time, are full of *blasphemy* against God.

presumption for his great army, and violent threats to destroy cities, and cut innocent men to pieces.

Change times and laws: the meaning of which is, that what God decrees is his law, and this prophecy contains it; an opposition by the *King of Prussia* to what God has decreed shall come to pass, his endeavouring by force of arms to stop the course of the prophecy, and change the decreed time for it to be fulfilled. The King of Prussia, by threatening, with the great strength of his army, to build up what God, to fulfil this prophecy, has thrown down; to restore that monarchy in France which God, to fulfil his recorded judgment in this prophecy, has removed for ever;—is the meaning of—*And he will think to change times and laws*.

And they will be given into his hand for a time and times, and the dividing of time. The meaning of which is, that the King of Prussia, although acting in opposition to the will of God (for every man that reads the Scripture, and believes it to be the book of truth, possesses from that moment a knowledge of good and evil, of right and wrong, of what is merciful, and what is cruel, of what is pleasing to God, and what is offensive) is permitted to wage a war of injustice against the righteous for three years and a half; during which time, according to the prophecy, he would conquer and destroy great multitudes of them. But my prayers prevailed with God, even against his own recorded judgment by Daniel; for I beseeched him to oppose the unjust designs of the king of Prussia before he invaded France; after he had, to suspend the prophecy, and for my sake to turn him back. The Lord God spoke to me in a vision, at night, and said " He shall go out of France with shame and confusion."

This promise was fulfilled in the year 1792; for, soon after the Prussian army entered France, God led it into such difficult places as to endanger its safety; he also sent the visitation of a wasting sickness, that forced it to go away, ashamed and highly disappointed. Although the other parts of the prophecy must necessarily be fulfilled to accomplish the purposes of God, and the destruction of the Prussian monarchy, the king cannot conquer as the judgment intended, but he is permitted to oppose, sometimes defeated with shame, and sometimes encouraged by deceitful success; until his armies become weak, and the Bear becomes strong; until the proper time arrives for him likewise to fall.

26 But the judgment shall sit (it ought to be, *But the judgment shall take place*) and they shall take away his dominion, to consume and to destroy it to the end.

The King of Prussia will have his country destroyed by *fire and sword*; his power will be taken away, and also his life: the government will be changed, and the monarchy will be abolished for ever.

In the year 1792 I sent the commands of God, as they were given to me by revelation at night, to the King of England, for the King of Prussia, before he invaded France, desiring him to return home, and have nothing to do with the people of that country; for the change of government taking place among them was determined, that the unalterable judgment of God, in the Scripture of Truth, might be fulfilled: reminding him, at the same time, as a corroborating testimony, that what I wrote was from God, of the monitor that entered his breast, and so powerfully struggled with his inclination to keep him back from war, that, when he positively resolved on it, reproached him strongly with the injustice.

That intelligent, internal monitor, was in truth no other than the compassionate spirit of the living God, striving, to the last moment, to save a falling man from the dreadful effects of his own judgment: but the King of Prussia despised the blessed intimation, and resolved on a war; that if there was no knowledge of God in the world, no part of human reason could find the least colourable pretence to justify.

At the time of my writing to the King of England, relative to the King of Prussia, I informed him, as I was commanded, of the certain failure of the combined armies of Prussia and Austria.

27 And the kingdom, and dominion, and the greatness, (meaning the power of all the kingdoms under the whole heaven,) will be given to the people and saints of the Most High: his kingdom is an everlasting kingdom, and all dominions must serve and obey him.

This is that real kingdom of heaven, of Christianity in practice, to believe and obey God, which was commanded by Christ, to preserve the soul of man, and a due knowledge of himself; preached by the apostles, though determined from the first transgression of Adam, and began more than seventeen hundred years ago, with all the materials ready prepared, from the multiplied interruptions of war and other causes, incident to human kingdoms, like the second temple of Jerusalem—long in building—This mighty structure is not finished yet. This is that stone, cut out without hands, mentioned by the prophet Daniel, in his second chapter, 34th and 35th verses, which breaks the head and the feet, the gold and the silver, the brass, the iron, and the clay, of the great image of human power to pieces: and this is that kingdom, mentioned by the same prophet, in the 44th verse following, which is to break in pieces and consume all other kingdoms; but which is to remain itself for ever. The name of this universal kingdom is Peace; it has the blessed Gospel for its government, and the Lord God for its king.

As I knew, in the beginning of 1792, that the King of England would enter into this war, and by doing so fall under the same judgment from God as the other monarchs shewn in the vision, unless I could, by a just explanation of the prophecies, persuade him to remain at peace; he will, I trust, with the queen and minister of state, do me the justice hereafter to acknowledge, that the danger was fully communicated; and that I did not cease in my endeavours to prevent him from joining in the confederacy against France, not only for a long time before he intended it, but also after he had, even till the designs of government were ready to be executed, by open preparations for hostility.

If this war was like any which has preceded it, a prince might, as usual, sit down at his leisure, and calculate, from his successes, how long to carry it on; or, by his defeats, how soon he must leave it off; but the death of Louis XVI. and the revolution in France, having proceeded from the recorded judgment of God, the two *things which have occasioned it, and which have rendered it so entirely different, that its consequences are already determined*, will be the same to the monarchs engaged in it, as it happens to a man unexpectedly caught in a large trap, on forbidden ground—the pains of death convince him of transgression before his eyes could warn him of the danger.

I know the judgments of God; by them I am directed; by revelation and through his holy Spirit I write. To fulfil, then, the seventh chapter of Daniel, and such parts of the revelation as mean the present time and the same things, the war now carrying on will involve all the nations engaged in it in great distress, and nearly all the princes of Europe in death. As I knew all this a considerable time before the war, I set my heart and my mind to intercede with God, although it was against his recorded judgments, to save the king, and *spare the country I live in*: I succeeded with God, and obtained an offer of mercy; but could not with man, to believe and accept it.

I wish well to the king and queen, and likewise their family; to know all that I have related, and more than I am permitted to tell; to know the unavoidable death of him, and afterwards the certain destruction of an amiable woman and her children, would, I thought, be a crime to reproach for ever the feelings of my heart, if I did not implore, when I knew the great kindness that God had for me, and endeavour, by all the means in my power, to prevent it.

But in doing this I have subjected myself to the power of human laws, when, indeed, I had the choice to make them subject to me; for if I had not become an intercessor, by prayer and supplication for the people I live among, I should have been sent away from London. Its fall would soon after take place; and then my revelation, as the next great thing to warn the world, would immediately succeed; but, preferring its safety to my own immediate advantage, *although informed at the time that the people would not believe; that I should be despised, and made suffer*; I obtained its pardon at the risque of my own life, and determined to remain in it until my time to be revealed was entirely completed.

I find, yes, I feel by dreadful experience, that all men are insensible to the consequences of those judgments, recorded in the Scripture, and are also exceedingly hardened against believing their true interpretation and time to be fulfilled. That I have suffered, by imprisonment and distress, more than is proper now to publish, *for entreating, when I was told that my entreaties were contrary to the prophecies*, to save the king and his family; London and its inhabitants, from recorded destruction; God, who is more generous to give mercy than man is grateful to believe and accept it, is by all this revealed knowledge of his prophecies my witness now, and will, in due time, in a short time, be additionally so, by terrible signs and mighty wonders.

I have said, in the first book, that the fullfilling of the judgment of God, however destructive they might prove to the nations or governments, which they are directed against, would not affect my personal safety, nor operate in the least to my prejudice: my elevation is recorded in the Scripture, and established by promise to myself; besides, I am not mortal to human power. But although I am to be great, *far above any prince on earth*, and cannot be destroyed by man: although the fall of governments and ruin of nations, will not be allowed to affect my personal safety, nor operate in the least to my prejudice, I will not provoke any, but endeavour, by a peaceable conduct, civility, and fair words, to make all men believe.

My earnest desire and prayer to God is, that as he has given me a pre-eminence of favour to all men that were ever upon earth before, I may be able, *although I have been in prison, insulted and despised; although my zeal is broke, and my inclination altered*, to save in this country one person as another; the king, as well as myself; the rich, as well as the poor; all without distinction. For which I request all men to meditate on the present times, and consult with themselves by their knowledge of the Scripture, by comparing the leading features of what ruined other great nations unexpectedly, to what are now as suddenly opening to human view, and what are as unexpectedly coming to pass in the world; of the judgments and prophecies to be fulfilled, which every man that has the spirit of conviction to believe, and an understanding to discern, must plainly perceive that the convulsed state of Europe, as it now presents itself, is one of their visible features; and that the sudden great war which occasions it, *Multiplying still as it lengthens against all forcible endeavours, deceiving when least expected and turning the prudent foresight of the wise politician to his own ruin*, is either the forerunning sign of general dissolution, or some other great and mighty thing.

Some of the prophecies which mean myself, and which I am commanded to insert.

THE PROPHET ISAIAH.

CHAP. IV.

1 And in that day, seven women shall take hold of one man, saying, We will eat our own bread, and wear our own apparel; only let us be called by thy name, to take away our reproach.

The man alluded to by the prophet is myself, and the time of the world is *just now come*. Remember that the seventh chapter of Daniel, and the sixth of the Revelation, are now fulfilling; remember, likewise, the second chapter and 24th verse of Haggai; by all of which, thrones are to fall, nation to be turned against nation, army against army, and man against man, until the earth is wasted of her people. By this great destruction of the human race, millions, millions of women will go to the grave widows, unmarried and barren.

The war is now, *compared to what it will be in future*—as four or five houses on fire, is to a large city set in flames by them: which all the arts and invention of the world, which all the force of power and political foresight cannot quench. It is from the great scarcity of mankind, which the war will occasion, that the prophet represents so many women as taking hold of one conspicuous and particular man.

2 In that day the branch of the Lord will be beautiful and glorious, and the fruit of the earth will be excellent and comely for them which are escaped of Israel.

3 And it shall come to pass, that he which is left in Zion, and he that remains in Jerusalem, shall be called Holy; even every one that is written among the living in Jerusalem.

4 When the Lord has washed away the filth of the daughters of Zion, and has purged the blood of Jerusalem from the midst of it, by the spirit of judgment and by the spirit of burning.

This verse alludes to the Jews after their restoration, and to Jerusalem in the latter time of the world, when rebuilt and inhabited; the Jews will then acknowledge Christ for their Messiah, and through the sanctification of his blessed Spirit they will be cleaned from sin.

5 And the Lord will create upon every dwelling-place of mount Zion, and upon her assemblies, a cloud and smoke by day, and the shining of a flame of fire by night; for upon all the glory (meaning the people) shall be a defence.

6 And there shall be a tabernacle for a shadow in the day time from the heat, and for a place of refuge, and for a covert from storm and from rain.

This is a figurative representation of the peace and safety of the Jews under the protection of God after their restoration to Jerusalem in 1798.

APOCRYPHA.—II. ESDRAS.

CHAP. XI.

36 Then I heard a voice which said to me, Look before thee, and consider the thing that thou seest.

37 And I beheld, and lo, as it were, a Roaring Lion chased out of the wood; and I saw that he sent out a man's voice to the eagle, and said,

This Roaring Lion, *as it were*, chased out of the wood, means myself: who am now forced out of concealment by divine command to rebuke the eagle; not her only, but the other princes likewise, if they will not believe what I write, and try to save themselves from the judgment of God, by sparing the effusion of human blood. This must necessarily be done to fulfil the prophecy, (*For it is a true one*) which is fully accomplished on my part by an explanation of the seventh chapter of Daniel, and declared aloud to the world by the publication of it in this book.

Peace being requested from God, and a suspension of his judgments offered through me, I earnestly request all the princes of Europe to forsake war, that they may enjoy the substantial blessings of long life, and everlasting happiness.

38 Hear thou, I will talk with thee, and the highest shall say to thee;

39 Art thou not it that remainest of the four beasts, whom I made to reign in my world, that the end of their times might come through them? (Instead of the word them, it should be, as it was in the original, Thee.)

40 And the fourth came, and overcame all the beasts,

fearfulness, and over the whole compass of the earth with much wicked oppression; and so long time dwelt he upon the earth with deceit.

41 For the earth hast thou not judged with truth.

42 For thou hast afflicted the meek, thou hast hurt the peaceable, thou hast loved liars, and destroyed the dwellings of them that brought forth fruit, and hast cast down the walls of such as did thee no harm.

43 Therefore thy wrongful dealing is come up to the Highest, and thy pride to the Mighty.

44 The Highest also has looked upon the proud times, and behold, they are ended, and their abominations are fulfilled.

45 And therefore appear no more, thou eagle: nor thy horrible wings, nor thy wicked feathers, nor thy malicious heads, nor thy hurtful claws, nor all thy vain body:

46 That all the earth may be refreshed, and may return, being delivered from thy violence; and that she may hope for the judgment and mercy of him that made her.

CHAP. XII.

10 And he said to me, This is the interpretation of the vision.

11 The eagle, whom thou saw come up from the sea, is the kingdom that was seen in the vision of thy brother Daniel.

12 But it was expounded to him, therefore now I declare it to thee.

I have inserted these verses not only as a demonstration of their truth, but likewise to shew the intimacy between the visions of Esdras and them of Daniel.

Moreover, when God was communicating by revelation at night a knowledge of this prophecy to me, he said, *in plain words as one man would speak to another; for it is in that manner all knowledge of what I write is first revealed to me.*) " I passed by this part with Daniel." It was mentioned as a confirmed certainty to me, that the *prophecy of* Esdras was given from a true vision.

31 And the lion, whom thou saw rising up out of the wood, and roaring, and speaking to the eagle, and rebuking her for her unrighteousness; with all the words which thou hast heard:

32 This is the Anointed (meaning myself, as prince of Israel) which the Highest hast kept for them, and for their wickedness to the end; he shall reprove them, and shall upbraid them with their cruelty.

33 For he shall set them before him alive in Judgment, and shall rebuke them and correct them.

34 For the rest of my people shall he deliver with mercy, those which have been preserved upon my borders, and he shall make them joyful until the day of judgment of which I have spoken to thee from the beginning.

CHAP. XIII.

25 This is the meaning of the vision, whereas thou saw a man coming up from the midst of the sea.

26 The same is he whom the Highest has kept a great season, which, by his ownself, (meaning in his own person,) shall deliver his people; (meaning his people the Jews) and he shall order them that are left behind.

I am the man alluded to in this chapter; coming from the sea, in the twenty-fith verse, is to signify that I should *as the person meant*, live on the ocean. I have; having been *in the English navy*; but am now rising from it, to fulfil this prophecy, that of Isaiah, Haggai, Jerimiah, Ezekiel, Daniel, Mallachi, and part of the Revelation to St. John likewise. For I was necessarily engaged with the sword, to fulfil the recorded judgment on the monarch I am to represent; and professionally a seaman, to fulfil the visions from God in this prophecy.

27 And whereas thou saw, that out of his mouth there came, as a blast of wind, and fire, and storm:

28 And that he had neither sword, nor any instrument of war; but that the rushing in of him destroyed the whole multitude that came to subdue him. This is the interpretation.

29 Behold, the days come when the Most High will begin to deliver them that are on the earth.

30 And he (*this means Christ, but the next verse, myself. For I am now his prophet and messenger: the branch of his family alluded to, and the designed signet of peace for all nations; the prince ordained to govern visibly for him in his city, and on his throne; therefore, he being God, Lord, and King, shews me to Esdras, as he did to St. John, spiritually repre-*

senting, and spiritually called under the name of his son, because universal dominion; as his empowered visible representative, immediately under himself, next to himself will be given to me) shall come to the astonishment of them that dwell on the earth.

31 And one shall undertake to fight against another, and one city against another; one place against another, one people against another, and one realm against another.

32 And the time shall be when these things shall come to pass, and the signs shall happen which I shewed thee before, and then shall my son be declared, whom thou saw as a man ascending.

33 And when all the people hear his voice, every man shall, in his own land, leave the battle they have one against another.

34 And an innumerable multitude shall be gathered together, as thou saw them, willing to come, and to overcome him by fighting.

35 But he shall stand upon the top of mount Sion.

36 And Sion shall come, and shall be shewed to all men, being prepared and builded, like as thou saw the hill graven without hands.

37 And this, my son, shall rebuke the wicked inventions of those nations, which for their wicked life, are fallen into the tempest;

38 And shall lay before them their evil thoughts, and the torments wherewith they shall begin to be tormented, which are like to a flame: and he shall destroy them without labour, by the law which is like to fire.

I recommend it to every person that reads this book, to take the Bible, and read from the beginning of the thirteenth chapter to the thirteenth verse, as it means myself: and likewise of the sixteenth chapter, from the eighteenth verse to the thirty-sixth, as it corroborates the prophecy of Isaiah, Daniel, and Haggai, relative to the immediate, and just now approaching, time of the world.

OF THE REVELATION.

CHAP. V.

The book means the prophecies intended to be concealed until this time of the world, which is the time they

Observe, the Revelation was given to St. John a long time after the death of Christ, not to commemorate those things which were before, which were fulfilled, and which were known before the time of writing it; but to record those things which are to be in future and which are to be fulfilled: according to the words of God, declared in the fourth chapter, and first verse, which are, "Come up hither, and I will shew thee the things which must be *hereafter.*" They were shewn to him in heaven, under such wonderful, such incomprehensible similitudes, in visions, as to seal their meaning a perfect secret, until the time of the world alluded to came, when the designed spiritual person (for no man can be a prophet of Christ, now under Christianity, and speaking through the Holy Ghost, his spirit, without bearing some similarity to himself in meekness and compassion; witness the apostles) would be revealed, to open the scriptural seals, and make known the secret prophecies under them in the book.

CHAP. VI.

The four first seals are opened, and the covering of secrecy is removed; the judgments which are to punish the world for transgression, by rising nation against nation, and man against man, are gone forth, *spiritually under the similitudes expressed in this chapter, to the eight verse,* and are begun to be fulfilled: the concealed meaning of the prophecies, which have been carefully preserved so for me until the present time, are now declared; the spiritual seals are opened, the contents of the spiritual book, which they shut, is known, and a revealed knowledge of it published in this *visible book,* for the good of all mankind.

The Lord God commands me to acknowledge the kindness of a poor woman, that brought me a three-penny loaf each week, every Monday morning, when I was in prison: Her name is Isabella Wake. The prison is Newgate.

A man that died the day before, of a bad fever, and from neglect, for the want of proper nourishment, as I was told, made a vacancy in a room, with fourteen poor men, little air, and much crouded, for me to come into his place.

The small, very small pennyworth of bread, with water

only, except one day in the week, when there are a few ounces of beef, for twenty-four hours, is barely sufficient to keep life and body together. The prison is very close; there is not room enough to promote health, by the necessary exercise of walking, there are no coals allowed for fire, nor candles for light. There is no bed to lie on, nor blanket to cover one: The poor are entirely destitute here.

When the condition of prisons, and the treatment of prisoners, is required for public information, it is from the poor man, whose health is injured by confinement who has to draw his little air through a small iron-barred window, who has but a small pennyworth of bread allowed for the whole day to live on, that a true account is to be received; but certainly not from the officers, keepers, and contractors, who live in plenty; whose emoluments swell in proportion as the prisons grow crouded.

Therefore be no longer astonished that London, in one part of the Revelation is called under the name of the great city, *for, she is the greatest city in Europe, and the richest in the world*; in another part she is called Sodom; and in a third, she is, as well as Rome, *spiritually called Babylon the Great*.

No man, who has any knowledge of God, can justly say, that London is without guilt, and her people are without sin; when her streets are full of vice, and her prisons are full of oppression.

ST. MATTHEW.

CHAP XXV.

37 Then shall the righteous answer him, saying, Lord, when saw we thee an hungred, and fed thee? or thirsty, and gave thee drink?

38 When saw we thee a stranger, and took thee in? or naked and clothed thee?

39 Or when saw we thee sick, or in prison and came to thee.

40 And the King will answer, and say to them, Verily I say to you, in as much as ye have done it to one of the least of these my brethren, ye have done it to me.

ISABELLA WAKE, this is the recorded testimony of your everlasting life, which I am commanded to give

[38]

Moreover, I will provide for you: and although I am now poor, without house or servant, I shall soon have abundance, and be at the head of the greatest nation on earth: In my palace you shall always have an apartment, and at my table you shall always have a seat.

I am commanded to acknowledge likewise the acts of friendship I received from Captain Hanchett, of Abingdon-street, which the Lord God considers as shewn directly to himself; therefore his blessing is on you; and by his promise in the Gospel, your reward is great. Moreover, I am commanded to inform you, as well as for the benefit of your children hereafter, as yourself immediately, that although your name is Hanchett, there is John Pitt Earl of Chatam, Sir Gilbert Elliott, and Charles Grey: you as well as them, the whole as well as myself, are of the Hebrews; branches of my own family, and are descended from David king of Israel.

All this has been told me by revelation, from the Lord God, in visions of the night.

There are many of my family, which have heard of me, and with which the Spirit of God has given me favour that do not want either inclination or ability to demonstrate their friendship; but they are deterred, from a fear of offending Government, and from a fear of incurring the imputation of guilt, by being generous.

The pre-ordained and designed signet of peace for all nations, cannot do any thing that will ultimately tend to injure any prince, government, or individual: if they view his words in a contrary light, it is because they calculate the future by the past; they know the things which were last month, but have no knowledge of those things which are to be the next. For all he does by writing, is to preserve the weak alive, and save the strong from falling down.

The weapons of his writing are not weak and carnal, but mighty and spiritual: when he is ordered to repronounce the judgments of God, and withdraw his eye from pity, the great power of his words will be felt to destroy, before their effects are seen to admonish; then, fleets, armies, princes, governments, and nations, must implore the God of heaven for mercy, and receive it likewise; or, they will, all that remain from the sword, be cut off by the sudden and irresistible falling of fire.

THE PROPHET MALACHI,

CHAP. IV.

5 Behold, I will send you Elijah the prophet, before the coming of the great and dreadful day of the Lord.

6 And he shall turn the heart of the fathers to their children, and the heart of the children to their fathers, lest I come, and smite the earth with a curse.

The Elijah, mentioned in this chapter, and the messenger, mentioned in the first verse of the third chapter, mean two distinct persons. The one was the immediate messenger of Christ, when he came for the salvation of mankind; the other, his recorded prophet, to pronounce his judgments, and warn the world, before he comes to destroy it.

This is that great prophet, alluded to in the last chapter, under the name of Elijah, and not St. John the Baptist: he will possess the Spirit of God equal to Elijah, and have the power of his fire in the same manner. He will turn the hearts of the fathers to the children, and the hearts of the children to the fathers; that is, he will suppress *war and violence*, which sets the old against the young, and the young against the old. He will command peace, and by the great power given him from heaven, enforce an obedience whereever he comes.

The appointment of this prophet, being to invite first, and compel after, all nations to come into the kingdom of peace, as a necessary preparation to meet Christ, when he comes to visit and judge the world: Saint John the Baptist, for being appointed to prepare for Christ, preaching the same kingdom of peace, and promising, by baptism, mercy to all that would believe, is the real and very reason, that Christ, in the seventeenth chapter of St. Matthew, calls him Elias.

At a former time, when I was entreating God to spare London, I mentioned no man by his title: but when I was writing an account of it for public information, he said to me " unless you write their titles, they themselves wont know who you mean." It will appear strange, because I am not acquainted with any of the distinguished persons alluded to; but I knew every one by some particular act that caught my approbation, and made me remember them then. It seemed as if God had done this on purpose, for he has often said to me since, in visions and revelations at night, You must be a wall of defence and safety to many a great man;—yes, even to some that despise you now. At that time, after mentioning the name of William Pitt, I passed by that of his brother; immediately after, the Lord God reminded me of it, and, in a voice of great softness and good nature, said, There is *John Pitt*, wont you mention him? You dont know who he is *I forgave*.

In the year of 1790 the Spirit of God begun first, (although I always had a presentiment of being some time or other very great,) to enlighten my understanding, and teach me to distinguish right from wrong. At that time I was an officer in the navy, and considering that voluntary swearing, which I was obliged to comply with every six months as a qualification to receive my pay, was unnecessary, unjust, and wicked, I requested to be indulged with permission to receive it without; stating at the same time, the concealed and unheeded cruelty of the oath, with my own reasons for objecting to the form: when I was told, in answer to my request, that there was an order of council to take the oath, and that it was not in the power of the admiralty to dispense with it.

Soon after this I made another request, supporting my objections to voluntary swearing, with observing, That if the *order of council* enforced an oath in any manner, or under any form whatever, and that the man it was directed to operate on, swore that he was not forced, but that the oath he took was a voluntary act—*the result of his own free will*—would it not in the sight of God in heaven, and every man of discernment under him on earth, amount to a false oath?

These reasons, with these objections, and the letter I received from the admiralty, stating their insufficient power to dispense with the usual form of swearing, I published at that time in the newspaper called the *Public Advertiser*.

During the time of my writing officially to the admiralty I had occasion to write also to the president, whom I knew to be a member of the council; with the business of swearing which led me to make an application, I remarked to him, That as men, whether few in number, or the encreased multitude of a senate were not infallible, they must consequently be subject to error. To corroborate more forcibly this assertion, and likewise to imprefs a conviction of its justice, I mentioned among other things a decision of the privy council, relative to a native of Glasgow, who had his ship seized in the West Indies for an *undesigned* infringement of the Navigation act.

After a legal investigation in that country, it was clearly proved and openly acknowledged, that although the apparent defect in the register might authorize the seizure, it could not justify a condemnation; because the commander, *like an honest man*, shewed it at the Custom-house, and received the approbation of the principal officer.

An appeal was lodged against this acquittal by the seizing officer in the West Indies, and brought before the Privy Council in England!—the ship was condemned.

To constitute a High Court of Equity, its members, to pronounce their judgment agreeable to that very name their existence as a court is derived from, must be governed more by the *intention* than the presumptive proof. But to constitute a Court of Law, its Judges must be directed by the express letter of the act of parliament under which they officiate.

For example, two men go into a forest; while the one is fetching a blow to cut down a tree, the axe flies from the handle and kills the other: Here is a presumptive proof of murder, and the law very justly brings the survivor to trial. But *equity*, viewing this circumstance in a proper light, declares the innocence, and acquits accordingly.

Another, and more relevant to the seizure. A man

acknowledged to be good and safe: after this, in consequence of some defect, it is declared illegal, and the holder subjected to a penalty.

I believe every man on earth, that has the common faculty of distinguishing white from black, will agree with me in saying, that it would be repugnant to equity to fine the holder for a defect he had no knowledge of as such, and for what was authorised by the very office of government that always issued the stamps.

The law supposes criminality from the appearance; but equity measures it from the design. The one is external and visible, provided many years before it may be wanted: the other is internal and spiritual, always alive in the heart of every judge that possesses prudence, learning, and penetration.

When I was writing of these things to the Earl of Chatham, on my knees I made a solemn vow to the Almighty God, declaring that if he would be pleased to enable me, I would most surely procure an indemnification for the poor man that lost his ship. Since that time the Lord God has told me, by revelation at night, That he would most truly enable me: for, if I liked, I should be President of the Council, and Chancellor of the Exchequer: I should have any thing that I required. Immediately after this, I heard another voice from heaven say, The Lord have mercy on them, if they had not you for their friend and counsellor; for England is the Spiritual Egypt mentioned in the 11th chapter of the Revelation to St. John.

After making the numerous representations I have mentioned, the Earl of Chatham, with great propriety, acknowledged their justice so far as to erase the word *Voluntary* from the prescribed form of swearing: but I was then reminded of the words of Christ in the 5th chapter, 34th verse, of St. Matthew, and strictly commanded to obey them. Soon after this, I requested from the Admiralty, and often repeated it, a dispensing order that I might receive my pay without an oath; but they would not grant it.

If the Earl of Chatham had shewn me the small favour I asked for, and certainly it would have been but a very small one to him, he should be held up to the world, as my friend, to be admired and regarded; he should wear such a durable coronet as would make him the envy of princes; it should be a coronet that no human power would ever be able to remove.

As the Admiralty would not give me that reasonable indulgence, I requested, as they would not shew me that kindness which, as men living by the navy, they might have done with ease, and without prejudice to their dignity, I wanted for a bit of bread to eat: I was besides treated so ill, as to be dragged to a workhouse without any legal authority, against every remonstrance I could make, and against every threat I could make use of to call them to a strict account for the injustice. The Admiralty knew all this; they might have prevented it, by ordering what was due to me to be paid; but they would neither prevent the evil, nor enable me to be liberated: they would not order the payment of what was due, until open falsehood was made use of to say I was out of my senses. It seemed as if they were under some private apprehension, though pleased with my distress, of being charged one day or other in the eyes of their country with unfeeling cruelty, and wanted some kind of colourable evidence to justify the proceeding.

' Hear, therefore, all nations, and be warned by it, what the Lord God has told me by revelation, and now commands me to write, that the injuries I received, because done for obeying his word in the blessed Gospel, the remembrance of them should never be blotted out from the throne of heaven. Moreover, he said likewise, That he would shake the English Admiralty as a man would violently bread in a basket, until he loosed the foundations of the earth, and shook the place in pieces.

If I am out of my senses, in the opinion of the Admiralty, for refusing, first to take an idle oath, secondly, a false one, and thirdly, to take any, Christ, the Saviour of the world, and him that Isaiah the prophet calls Wonderful Counsellor, who prohibits by his Gospel in the strongest terms all kind of swearing, must, by the same rule of knowledge for giving such a command, be out of his.

As the Quakers never swear, and their objections to it are sanctioned by a just indulgence of law; they, the king and parliament, for giving the indulgence, must, for the same reason as I am, be out of theirs.

Chrift having been abufed at Jerufalem, reproached with having a devil, being mad, and out of his fenfes, makes it the lefs aftonifhing for me, that am his fervant, to be reviled in the fame manner: For which the Lord God commands me to remind all men, from the teftimony of his bleffed Gofpel, that the fin is blafphemy againft his Holy Spirit, and that the punifhment is everlafting fire.

It is from vifions and revelations, and through the Holy Ghoft, that I write this book for the benefit of all men: therefore, to fay it is falfe, that I am mad, am an impofter, have a devil, or am out of my fenfes, conftitutes the dangerous fin of blafphemy.

ST. MATTHEW,

CHAP. XII.

31 Wherefore I fay to you, All manner of fin and blafphemy fhall be forgiven to men; but the blafphemy againft the Holy Ghoft fhall not be forgiven unto men.

32 And whofoever fpeaks a word againft the Son of Man, it fhall be forgiven him; but whofoever fpeaks againft the Holy Ghoft, it fhall not be forgiven him, neither in this world, neither in the world to come.

ST. MATTHEW,

CHAP. V.

22 But I fay to you, that whofoever is angry with his brother without a caufe, fhall be in danger of the judgment: and whofoever fhall fay to his brother, Raca, fhall be in danger of the council: but whofoever fhall fay, Thou fool, fhall be in danger of hell fire.

To infult any perfon, whether high or low, rich or poor, of whatever fect or denomination, that preaches or writes through the Holy Ghoft, which is indeed the true Spirit of God, by faying that he is foolifh, courage acts of injuſtice, or diſturb ſociety, by promoting violence in any manner whatſoever.

From the Spirit of God flows all the good things which are neceſſary to encreaſe the life of man, and unite all nations under the Goſpel bond of Chriſtianity and friendſhip; they conſiſt of love, peace, civility, and kindneſs; by a ſtrict attention to obſerve the good ſpirit that encourages theſe things, may be eaſily diſcerned from the evil one that oppoſes them.

ST. PAUL TO THE EPHESIANS,

CHAP. IV.

29 Let no corrupt communication proceed out of your mouth, but that which is good to the uſe of edifying, that it may miniſter grace to the hearers.

30 And grieve not the Holy Spirit of God, whereby ye are ſealed to the day of redemption.

31 Let all bitterneſs, and wrath, and anger, and clamour, and evil ſpeaking, be put away from you, with all malice.

32 And be ye kind to one another, tender-hearted, forgiving one another, even as God, for Chriſt's ſake, has forgiven you.

The Lord Jeſus Chriſt, the better to prevent the commiſſion of ſin, and the fall of man, for there is no ſaviour but him, begins with ſtrictly prohibiting the leſſer but poiſonous names of flattery and falſehood, that they ſhould not, by a frequency of uſe, corrupt the mind, and encreaſe to the more dangerous ones of blaſphemy and rebellion.

FIRST OF THESSALONIANS,

CHAP. V.

19 Quench not the Spirit.
20 Deſpiſe not prophecyings.
21 Prove all things; hold faſt that which is good.
22 Abſtain from all appearance of evil.
23 And the very God of Peace ſanctify you wholly: and I pray God that your whole ſpirit, and ſoul, and body, may be preſerved blameleſs to the coming of our Lord Jeſus Chriſt.

CORINTHIANS,

CHAP. II.

12 Now we have received, not the spirit of the world, but the spirit which is of God; that we might know the things which are freely given to us of God.

13 Which things also we speak, not in the words which man's wisdom teaches, but which the Holy Ghost teaches; comparing spiritual things with spiritual.

14 But the natural man receives not the things of the Spirit of God, for they are foolishness to him; neither can he know them, because they are spiritually discerned.

15 But he that is spiritual judges all things; yet he himself is judged of no man.

COLOSSIANS.

CHAP. II.

8 Beware, lest any man spoil you through philosophy and vain deceit, after the tradition of men, after the rudiments of the world, and not after Christ.

No man ought to advance the writings or opinion of another to assist his own, when what he says is proved to be in opposition to the words of Christ; neither ought he to go back to the Law, which was for the Jews alone, in their own country, to look for a precedent, to favour his delusive method of reasoning, when the thing he wants to justify is quite contrary to the blessed Gospel of peace and salvation.

The following are the words of St. Paul, in the fourteenth chapter to the Corinthians, which I am commanded to insert, as justly applicable to many at this time; when some, possessing all spiritual knowledge, as they thought, exalted themselves against him, and doubted the spiritual truth of what he said.

VERSE XXXVII.

If any man thinks himself to be a prophet, or spiritual, let him acknowledge that the things I write to you are the commands of the Lord.

38 But if any man be ignorant, let him be ignorant. That is, if any man is not spiritual to discern the works

of the Spirit of God, let him conceal his ignorance; let him not speak againſt them, becauſe he has not the Spirit to difcern, faith to believe, or knowledge to comprehend their truth.

GALATIANS,

CHAP. I.

6 I marvel that ye are ſo ſoon removed from him that called you into the grace of Chriſt to another goſpel;

7 Which is not another; but there is ſome that trouble you, and would pervert the Goſpel of Chriſt.

8 But though we, or an angel from heaven, preach any other goſpel to you than that which we have preached to you, let him be accurſed.

9 As we ſaid before, ſo ſay I now again, if any man preach any other goſpel to you than that ye have received, let him be accurſed.

SECOND OF THESSALONIANS,

CHAP. I.

Seeing it is a righteous thing with God to recompence tribulation to them that trouble you;

7 And to you, who are troubled, reſt with us, when the Lord Jeſus ſhall be revealed from heaven, with his mighty angels,

8 In flaming fire, taking vengeance on them that know not God, and that obey not the goſpel of our Lord Jeſus Chriſt.

9 Who ſhall be puniſhed with everlaſting deſtruction from the preſence of the Lord, and from the glory of his power.

It is time to awaken all nations from their ſleep of deluſive ſecurity, by informing them, that the time alluded to by St. Paul, in his Second Epiſtle to the Theſſalonians, is come; and that there is a great falling away from an obedience to the bleſſed Goſpel. And likewiſe to inform them that Satan has been revealed; the age of the world is great, and the time is come for it; he is now allowed more power, becauſe ſin is encreaſed, to influence and deceive man than at any time ever before. I am the prophet to whom the miniſter of ſin was revealed; he is a ſpirit, and no man can ſee him in the open day-light, unless sanctified by the power of the Holy Ghost, and his eye-sight strengthened for the purpose.

It is for this reason that I am the appointed witness for God, and his last recorded prophet, to warn all nations, and desire them to obey the blessed Gospel of salvation.

The following are some more of the visions, *which God shewed me, and which I am commanded to publish here.*

IN the month called July, 1791, I was in a vision, and was carried away, by the Spirit of God, to the sea coast, in the English channel—a new ridge of unknown land was brought in an instant plain to my eyes, while the finger of a hand wrote, in large capital letters, with great quickness, and a voice pronounced twice from heaven at the same time,

SWEDE, SWEDE!

After this I was in a vision in the month of January 1792, and was carried away by the Spirit of God to Sweden, when I was made look through a window in a room; I did, and saw a man walk from the side of a great chair, leaving it empty. I could not see his face as he went away, and although I could not, nor perceive that he had committed any crime, I thought with myself that he had been doing wrong. Immediately the angel that stood by me said, The chair means the chair of state; and that man you saw will make it empty. The King of Sweden is *delivered over for death*, and that is the very man that will shoot him.

The prince of Orange is closely pursued likewise, but he is not delivered over yet.

After this I was in a vision, and saw the Prussian eagle perched on a chair of state; soon after, on a sudden, I saw the chair, the house, and the whole city where the chair stood, in flames. The angel that was near me, said, He is likewise pursued now.

After this I was in a vision, and the Lord God talked with me, and said, I give you the life of the Swede; but know this for certain, that if you prevent his death, the man himself will not believe there was any danger of it. And when you write hereafter of things in this country, you will be called an imposter, a fool, and a liar; you will be imprisoned, and treated very ill. When I see this, it will make me angry; I will then begin to kill the people, and I will surely destroy this city.

For which I gave no public information to warn the king of Sweeden, and prevent his death. Had this man lived, he would have commanded the German army against France; his private plan was to go through Normandy, close by the sea-coast, to be supplied the easier with provisions from England, and endeavour, by all possible means, to take the harbour of Brest.

He said to himself, in his own closet, This is the plan I will pursue; it will be giving a mortal blow to the French navy, and getting a safe harbour for our own ships.

All this was made known to me by revelation from the Lord God, and which I communicated to the queen and minister of state in 1792, some time before the provinces of Brittany and Normandy shewed any open apppearance of hostility against the present government of France.

In the month of April 1793, I was in a vision, and was carried away in the spirit of God to Russia, where I saw a Bear stop and rest itself under a large tree; soon after I beheld a man, that lay concealed among the branches, drop down softly, and with a sharp piece of iron, which he held in his hand, stab the Bear; pronouncing, as he did so, I have watched a long time for you, but now I have caught you at last.

I know by revelation from the Lord God, that this vision means the present empress of Russia; for which, being permitted, I give her this warning.

Let the death of the kings of Sweeden and France, which is but a little time past; the death of the king of Spain and another, which will soon take place, for they are pursued; convince the princes and the people of Europe, that the seventh chapter of Daniel and the second of Haggai are now fulfilling.

At a former time when the Lord God was instructing

On the 3d of March, 1794, I was in a vision, and saw the sun in its full strength, clear and high up in the firmament: soon after I saw another sun rise on a sudden, equally large as the former, and stand close by it; both shone with equal brightness, and the last as well as the first, enlightened the world.

After the first division of this copy was sent to be printed, and even some of it done, the printer was advised not to do it according to my form; for, if he did, prosecution, imprisonment, and perhaps hanging would be the consequence to him. For which the Lord God commands me to keep back the additional information that otherways would be given, and terminate the book.

I have said already that the sixth chapter of the Revelation was now fulfilling: the *four first seals* are opened and the covering, which kept the meaning of the prophecies a profound secret until the present time, is removed: the *recorded* decrees are held up, and God himself commands a knowledge of their contents to be published for the good of all nations. But if I cannot have the commands of God, and a knowledge of his judgments, printed exactly as I write, how is this extension of mercy to be known over Europe, and the people of London informed of any danger that is past, or any danger that is to come? All the prophecies in the Scripture were given through men: the Ninevites were warned through one.

How is the king to save himself from that *recorded*, determined and unavoidable death, which all the powers of armies cannot prevent? How is London and the parliament to be saved, when they are recorded in the Scripture of truth to be destroyed? How is England, Europe, and most parts of the world to be saved, when they are recorded to he filled with blood by war, and to be made desolate for ever by earthquakes, if the person I employ is deterred, by the fears of prosecution and evil from printing the full copy, exactly as I give it?

The king of Egypt and his people were destroyed because they would not believe Moses but the king of Nineveh; and his people were saved, because they did believe Jonnah, and reform.

The king of England, the chancellor of the Exchequer, secretaries of state, other members of administration and as many members of both houses of parliament, as my ablity will allow; the bishops, judges, and all the foreign ambassadors in London: will have a book sent to each.

On account of my being insulted, because the Jews do not believe in the first book, by a public acknowledgment of it, the Lord God commands me to remind all men of what is wrote in that book, and to say that as the Jews do not believe in Christ, it cannot be expected that they will in me; *neither are they,* until I am revealed in a similar manner to Moses in Egypt, but with the additional power of fire as his sign, to make them.

The night before I had finished this book for the press, the Lord God shewed it to me in a vision, ready printed, holding it up at the same time by one leaf, and shaking all the others open, while he pronounced, in strong clear words, and commanded me to write them down exactly as he spoke, for universal information:

There is nothing in this book that the English law can take hold of:—So says Him that Isaiah the prophet calls Wonderful Counselllor.

I request every body in all nations, to read this book with attention, and receive it favourably; for although the information and warning it contains is through me, yet it is not mine, but God's.

RICHARD BROTHERS.

London, No. 57, Paddington Street,
11 of the month, called April 1794.

SOME OF THE PROPHECIES

Which mean myself, and which I am commanded to insert, the appointed time being now fulfilled.

DEUTERONOMY,

CHAP. XVIII.

15 The Lord thy God will raise up unto thee a prophet, from the midst of thee, of thy brethren, like unto me; unto him ye shall hearken.

16 According to all thou desiredst of the Lord thy God in Horeb, in the day of the assembly, saying, Let

me not hear again the voice of the Lord my God; neither let me see this great fire any more that I die not.

The time of the world alluded to by Moses, though not expresly mentioned in this chapter, when a prophet would be raised up, to order the restoration of the children of Israel in the latter days, (for he was fully informed of all the calamities *that would befal them, afterwards their deliverance and return, to be disperfed no more*, as the thirty-second chapter sufficiently testifies,) is the present; and myself the man—the designd prophet, as leader of the Jews, tofulfil a similar character, according to his own words, *like unto me*.

For Christ is the head of all prophecy; from him flows the Divine Spirit of truth: he is Lord and God; he is all that Isaiah says of him—The Wonderful Counsellor, the Mighty God, the Everlasting Father, the Prince of Peace.

Moses was but a man, and to a man like himself he alludes; as the Lord himself likewise declares in the three following verses.

17 And the Lord said to me, They have well spoken that which they have spoken;

18 I will raise them up a prophet from among their brethren, like unto thee; and I will put my words in his mouth, and he shall speak to them all that I command him.

19 And it shall come to pass, that whosoever will not hearken to my words, which he shall speak in my name, I will require it of him.

The Testimony given by St. Matthew *the apostle, of who* Christ *was.*

CHAP. I.

22 Now all this was done, that it might be fulfilled, which was spoken of the Lord, by the prophet, saying,

23 Behold, a virgin shall be with child, and shall bring forth a son, and they shall call his name Emanuel; which, being interpreted, is God with us.

The Testimony of St. John *the Apostle.*

CHAP. I.

1 In the beginning was the word, and the word was with God, and the word was God.

2 The same was in the beginning with God.

3 All things were made by him; and without him was not any thing made that was made.

4 In him was life; and the life was the light of men. And the light shone in darkness; and the darkness comprehended it not. There was a man sent from God, whose name was John.

7 The same came for a witness, to bear witness of the light, that all men through him might believe. He was not that light, but was sent to bear witness of that light. That was the true light, which lighteth every man that comes into the world.

10 He was in the world, and the world was made by him, and the world knew him not.

11 He came to his own, and his own received him not; but as many as received him, to them gave he power to become the sons of God. Which were born, not of blood, nor of the will of the flesh, nor of the will of man, but of God.

14 And the word was made flesh, and dwelt among us, &c.

The Testimony given by St. Paul, I. *Timothy,*

CHAP. III.

16 And without controversy, great is the mistery of godliness; God was manifest in the flesh, justified in the Spirit, seen of angels, preached to the Gentiles, believed on in the world, and received up into glory.

The meaning of this Chapter having been almays misunderstood by expounders of the Scripture, I am commanded to insert and explain it for the benefit of all men.

ACTS.—Chap. VII.

29 Then fled Moses at this saying, and was a stranger in the land of Midian, where he begat two sons.

36 And when forty years were expired, there appeared to him in the wilderness of mount Sina, an angel of the Lord in a flame of fire in a bush.

31, 32 Saying, I am the God of thy fathers, &c.

37 This is that Moses, which said to the children of Israel, a prophet shall the Lord your God raise up unto you, of your brethren like unto me.

This is he *(meaning Moses still, and not the prophet alluded to in the preceding verse; who was not Christ, neither, as has always been erroneously supposed)* that was in the church, (meaning the tabernacle) in the wilderness *with the angel* which spoke *to him* in mount Sina.

39 To whom our fathers would not obey, (meaning Moses) but thrust him from them, (meaning Moses often did, he fast, and pray, that God might not destroy the congregation,) and in their hearts turned back again into Egypt.

Who was the conspicuous person that the angel constantly accompanied, manifested himself to, and talked with during forty years in the wilderness, according to the 38th verse, but Moses? Who did the angel speak to in mount Sina from a flame of fire in a bush? St. Stephen meant no other here than Moses.

40 Saying to Aaron, make us Gods to go before us; as for this Moses, which brought us out of the land of Egypt, we know not what is become of him.

Expounders of the Scriptures have always supposed that St. Stephen, by repeating in this chapter the verses I have inserted from Deuteronomy, meant Christ to be the prophet alluded to by Moses, which is, like himself, to collect and lead home the Jews; but he does not; he repeats it as an historical account, to remind the council, before which he stood for judgment, that as their fathers had before rejected Moses in the wilderness, so did they their children reject Christ at Jerusalem. But in no one part does he, or St. Peter in the 3d chapter, mean that Christ is the prophet alluded to by Moses in the eighteenth chapter of Deuteronomy,—*as the fortieth verse sufficiently testifies.*

REVELATION TO ST. JOHN,

CHAP XII.

St. John the Apostle in this chapter describes a woman as cloathed with the sun, *the moon under her feet (meaning darkness*, or *the Turkish empire in Asia*), and a crown of twelve stars on her head. The sun alluded to is not the sun in the firmament, neither is that sun the Lord Jusus Christ, as has been always erroneously supposed. The woman is not the church, nor yet the Blessed Virgin, the mother of Christ, as has always been likewise erroneously supposed; but that sun means an entire man, composed of flesh and blood like any other; and that woman the princess of Israel. The prince is represented as a sun, because that through him God will enlighten the world with more knowledge than ever it had yet, and give a fresh manifestation of his mercy to prolong its duration. The woman, as his consort, is represented as clothed with him, and also as wearing a crown of twelve stars, because he, as her husband, is prince of the twelve tribes.

The child, *who will govern all nations immediately under and next to God*, being caught up to God and to his throne, means no more than the child going up to Jerusalem, where the throne of God will be on earth. The woman's going into the wilderness, means going up to Jerusalem also; the words into the wilderness are mentioned, because the city is situated *far inland* from the sea. The dragon means a European prince now alive, who will pour out proclamations and manifestoes after me, as a flood would issue from the mouth of a dragon: *for Satan will be in him.*

At the time God was explaining this chapter to me, he said, when I give you power to destroy that man from the face of the earth, you will melt into pity and spare his life; for which all my people will universally blame you, because he is their enemy and oppressor. Those strange names are given, and those difficult allusions to be understood, are made by St. John on purpose to seal the true meaning of the prophecies and revelation an entire secret, *according to the 5th chapter*; untill the full time is accomplished, and the appointed person made known to publish them to the world.

The prophet Ezekiel in the visions of God to him, describes the great extent, and grandeur of Jerusalem at a future time; and likewise of its being governed by a human prince.

This is the very man, *the appointed of God*, that is now abused, and publicly reproached in London—*the capital of the spiritual Egypt, as is mentioned by St. John in the 11th chapter*, with being a hypocrite, and a fanatic impostor.

Remember thofe things, O my God; and as thy thunder on the 7th of this month—Auguft—was to fhew thy full determination to throw down cities, and dafh in pieces the council of evil men, if they committed any violence against me, *for otherways I fhould now be lying in the common prifon*—So, O my God, execute; for they have no faith to believe thy juft judgments, nor charity to be civil to thy meffenger that declares thy great offers of mercy.

Firft publifhed Auguft the 10th, 1794.

THE reafon why thefe parts of Scripture, and the other things which follow, were not inferted when the firft edition of this book was printed, is, the time was not accomplifhed, and the Lord my God would not permit them to be publifhed until it was.

I am now commanded to make them publicly known for the information and b nefit of all men: In obedience to which, as his fervant and prophet, I do.

SECOND OF SAMUEL,

CHAP. XXII.

44. Thou alfo haft delivered me from the ftrivings of my people, (meaning the then children of Ifrael, over whom David was king) Thou haft kept me to be head of the Heathen: a people which I know not fhall ferve me.

This promife to king David then, meant that it fhould be fulfilled to him in his defcendant at a future time; a man, a human being, like any other that is compofed of flefh and blood; but not the Lord Jefus Chrift, who is God; who always was, and always will be, the head of the Heathen, and all nations. The promife was made from God to David, to be fully accomplifhed in that man's defcendant; which defcendant is myfelf; I fhall, under God, rule all nations under the government of the Gofpel to fulfil that covenant to David, and the promife

46 Strangers shall fade away, and they shall be afraid to come out of their close places.

47 The Lord lives, and blessed be my rock: and exalted be the God—the rock of my salvation.

48 It is God that avengeth me; and that brings down the people under me; and that brings me forth from my enemies.

49 Thou also hast lifted me up on high, above them that rise up against me: thou hast delivered me from the violent man.

50 Therefore I will give thanks to thee, O Lord, *among the Heathen*, and I will sing praises to thy name.

Here, David, who was not himself among the Heathen, was praising God for his descendant that should have this promise fulfilled to him, and who should be among the Heathen.

51 He (meaning the Lord) is a Tower of Salvation for his king: (meaning the descendant of David as king, ruling over all nations under the covenant and constant direction of God,) and sheweth mercy to his Anointed, unto David, and to his seed for evermore.

That Christ, the Saviour of the world, should be born of a Virgin, and that he should be called the Wonderful Counsellor, the Mighty God, the Everlasting Father, and the Prince of Peace, Isaiah the prophet sufficiently testifies: that Christ was so born, St. Matthew the Apostle witnesses in the first chapter of that part of the Gospel wrote by him. And Christ himself says in the 22d chapter when speaking to the Pharisees,—" What think ye of Christ? Whose son is he? They say to him, The son of David. He says to them, How then does David in Spirit call him Lord, saying, the Lord said to my Lord, sit thou on my right hand, till I make thy enemies thy footstool? if David then call him Lord, how is he his son? and no man was able to answer him a word; neither durst any man, from that day forth, ask him any more questions."

The words are, " Unto David and to his seed for evermore."

It means, to continue in succession from father to son, from the one as a man, to the other as a man, while the world lasts.

The Blessed Virgin Mary, *through whom Christ the Redeemer, who was God, came into the world*, was descended from king David: it is for this that Christ, though he was the Everlasting Father and Creator of all things, is alluded to as the son of David.

Mary was first cousin to that Joseph, who was promised to be her husband when found with child by the Holy Ghost. *St. Matthew chapter 1st.* Both Mary and Joseph were descended from one grandfather, who was Matthan; she the daughter of one brother, and Joseph the son of the other. *Told me by revelation from the Lord God.*

ZACHARIAH,

CHAP. VIII.

20 Thus says the Lord of Hosts, It shall yet come to pass, that there shall come people, and the inhabitants of many cities; and the inhabitants of one city shall go to another, saying, Let us go speedily to pray before the Lord, and to seek the Lord of Hosts; I will go also.

22 Yea, many people and strong nations shall come to seek the Lord of Hosts in Jerusalem, and to pray before the Lord.

23 Thus says the Lord of Hosts; In those days it shall come to pass, that ten men shall take hold out of all languages of the nations, even shall take hold of the skirt of him that is a Jew, saying, We will go with you; for we have heard that God is with you.

The time of the world, meant by the prophet, when this would be fulfilled, is at the restoration of the Jews, in the latter days; and myself the conspicuous particular Jew, as leader of the Jews, alluded to. I shall be importuned by many out of all nations, when revealed comparatively taking hold of my skirt, entreating to go with me to Jerusalem; because God, the mighty power of his Spirit, and fire, will be with me.

More of the VISIONS *which God shewed me, and which I am now commanded to publish.*

IN the month called June, 1791, at the hour of two in the afternoon, I saw a hand, from the wrist downwards, like the hand of a man, with the fore-finger pointed out, appear on a sudden a little above the height of my head, near the door, on the wall or partition of the room I was then in. After this I was infored, by revelation, at night, from the Lord God, that it meant the speedy end of the present King of England and his empire, like Belshazzar and Babylon, both of which would soon be destroyed.

In the month called May, 1792, I was in a vision, and receiving instruction from God of future things: he shewed me the queen, greatly alarmed at his judgments, by my revelation, with the power of fire, and immediately she cried out, The Lord have mercy on us! we shall all be destroyed! we shall all be destroyed!

After this I was in a vision again, and the Lord God shewed me the present Queen of England, coming towards me, slow, trembling, and afraid. This was communicated, with other things, to William Pitt, in the month called June, 1792. And likewise informing him, at the same time, that it would most certainly be fulfilled: it will; it is established with God, and will be so.

In the beginning of the month of June, 1792, I was in a vision, and was carried away, by the Spirit of God, to the palace called St. James's, where I saw the present King of England; he rose from his seat on seeing me, and immediately sent me his own magnificent star, at the same time breathing on it, and kissing, as if kissing to take a last farewell; yet not with grief and reluctance to give, but with evident satisfaction. Why the King of England should take his own conspicuous ornament and send it to me, was a thing that I was greatly astonished at; I wished to know the meaning, but could not discover, until a loud voice pronounced down from heaven, The Lord God delivers his life over into your hands, and he will give you any thing to preserve it. This vision, with others, and other things, was communicated, by Divine command, to the king, in 1792. The letter which contained it, with others to the King, the Queen, and the Chancellor of the Exchequer, were put into the penny post-office, to be sent by that conveyance, according to the directions I received on that head by revelation from God.

1794. This day, called Thursday, and the 12th of the month called June, I was in a vision, at the hour of two in the afternoon, when the Lord God spoke to me in a voice of great quickness, carrying me away to the Bank of England at the same time, and saying, There is one of twenty. The whole place rung and trembled with the clear but sharp sound of his words. It is by his sacred and particular command I mention this vision in writing.

The 13th, in the morning, the Lord God said to me, among other things, in a vision, You see those people do not believe, neither will they for all your endeavours; why then do you continue to entreat me for them?

The 14th, in the morning, the Lord God spoke to me, and said, The judgment is now against this nation; the thunder, just past, was to proclaim it: Pharaoh is appointed to die, and his government to be destroyed; the priests, and all the abominable idolatries of Egypt, shall perish, never to be found any more.

In the same manner that the Lord God spoke to the prophet Samuel, and revealed a knowledge of his designs, in the same manner also he speaks to me, and reveals a knowledge of his will.

FIRST OF SAMUEL.

CHAP. III.

1 And the child Samuel ministered unto the Lord before Eli, and the word of the Lord was precious in those days; there was no open vision.

2 And it came to pass at that time, when Eli was laid down in his place, and his eyes began to wax dim, that he could not see, and ere the lamp of God went out in the temple of the Lord, where the ark of God was, and Samuel was laid down to sleep,

4 That the Lord called Samuel; and he answered, Here am I. And he ran unto Eli, and said, Here am I; for thou calledst me. And he said, I called not; lie down again. And he went and lay down.

6 And the Lord called yet again, Samuel. And Samuel arose, and went to Eli, and said, Here am I;

for thou didſt call me. And he anſwered, I called not, my ſon; lie down again.

7 Now Samuel did not yet know the Lord, neither was the word of the Lord yet revealed to him.

8 And the Lord called Samul again the third time. And he aroſe, and went to Eli, and ſaid, Here am I; for thou didſt call me. And Eli perceived that the Lord had called the child.

9 Therefore Eli ſaid to Samuel, Go, lie down; and it ſhall be, if he call thee, that thou ſhalt ſay, Speak, Lord; for thy ſervant heareth. So Samuel went and lay down in his place.

10 And the Lord came and ſtood, and called, as at other times, Samuel, Samuel. Then Samuel anſwered, Speak, Lord; for thy ſervant heareth. And the Lord ſaid to Samuel, Behold, I will do a thing in Iſrael, at which both the ears of every one that heareth it ſhall tingle.

12 In that day I will perform againſt Eli all things which I have ſpoken concerning his houſe: when I begin, I will alſo make an end.

1794. The 25th of the month called June, the Lord God ſaid to me, in a viſion of the night, on my bed, in ſeven days more the judgment will be on this nation.

After this I was in a viſion, and the Lord God brought cloſe to me, that I might hear the report of a gun that was fired, and ſee a man privately ſhoot at another, to kill him: it was ſo near, that I ſaw the flaſh, and ſmelt the powder. Before the death of the King of Sweden, I was ſhewn, in a viſion, ſimilar to this, that he would be delivered over from the protection of God, to be ſhot.

I know, becauſe the Lord God has explained it to me by revelation, that this viſion means the man fired at to be the preſent King of England. He will be ſhot, but not killed; he will be wounded, but not mortaly.

He has not believed me at any time, although I fully informed him in 1792, and ſince, that it would be ſo: neither will he, until the very evil is viſited on him: and viſited on him to increaſe his diſtreſs, at a time when he is ſurrounded with danger, and loaded with trouble; it moſt certainly will. Then the King of England will be convinced, by woeful and feeling proofs, but it will be very late;—comparatively, when Death knocks at the door, that he defpifed the ofered mercy of God in 1792, and conftantly fince his beft friend, among mankind, as falfe.

In the month called March, 1794, I was in a vifion, and the Lord God fhewed me a large and very tall oak tree; it ftood alone; it was entirely withered, and all its branches were cut off. While I was confidering the tree, its lonely condition and nakednefs, I heard a very loud voice call out of heaven, Hew down that tree. Immediately the tree was covered with a thick cloud of darknefs, and an angel defcended from God, who ftruck the tree with fo violent a blow that it fell to the ground, and in its fall it made a great noife.

1794. Firft of the month called July, the Lord God faid to me, among other things, in a vifion, early in the morning (for I had been earneftly praying to him the evening before, to haften my revelation to the Jews, and inform me how long it would be until it took place; beacufe I was daily abufed as an impoftor, for publifhing his commands, by wicked men; every one of them led on under the influence of an evil fpirit)—You muft be at Conftantinople, in your way to Jerufalem, by this time the next year.

The 2d of the fame month, the Lord God faid to me, in a vifion on my bed, early in the morning, in breaking bread, you muft not any longer fay to any perfon, Peace and friendfhip, but falvation only to the fpiritual.

I know, by revelation, that Chriftopher Love, a clergyman, who was unjuftly tried, condemned, and put to death in London, in the year of 1651, had the Divine Spirit of the living God, and prophecied from it. He teftified of me at that time under different names, though all of them meant one and the fame perfon; that of a Bright Star, as a Sound of Thunder in the Ears of the Wicked, a Lantern to the Jews, and a Great Man.

The Lord God commands me to give this teftimony, and alfo to fay, that he will foon fend, in anger, the vifitation of his judgment on London, and call her to a ftrict account for fhedding not only the blood of this righteous man, but likewife all his other faithful witneffes,

I know likewise, by revelation from the Lord God, and am commanded to write it down, that John Maximilian Daut was sanctified by the divine Spirit of Truth, and prophecied, under its sacred direction, in the year of 1709. He has also testified of me under different names.

The Lord God commands me to inform you, John Wright, that you are of the Hebrews, of the tribe of Levi, descended from Aaron the high priest, by Phinehas, Zadok, and Ezra; for which the covenant to your forefather, Phinehas, of an everlasting priesthood, is renewed, given to you, to be manifested in you.

NUMBERS,

CHAP. XXV.

10 And the Lord spake unto Moses saying,

11 Phinehas, the son of Eleazar, the son of Aaron the priest, hath turned my wrath away from the children of Israel, while he was zealous for my sake among them, that I consumed not the children of Israel in my jealousy.

12 Wherefore say, Behold I give to him my covenant of peace:

13 And he shall have it, and his seed after him; even the covenant of an everlasting priesthood; because he was zealous for his God, and made an atonement for the children of Israel.

This is the recorded testimony which the Lord my God commands me to give; and to say to you likewise, You are sanctified by the Holy Ghost, the divine spirit of Truth.

The Lord God commands me to say to all you, professing Christianity, whom I have, by his sacred direction, acknowledged to be of the Hebrews, descended from Israel; for you, and your children after you, are some of his chosen people; not to take up, in obedience, to any law or any human power whatever, warlike arms, to shed blood, or commit violence, in consequence of the approaching calamities which he will most surely bring on this Egyptian land.

Neither mind the people that blaspheme God, and revile you for believing in his teftimonies: the wicked have always rofe againft the righteous, and this land like Egypt of old, has many tafk-mafters to abufe and opprefs in it. Therefore comfort yourfelves in the knowledge of the promifes of God to his fervants: For I declare, by his facred command, that the vifible Jews are but few in number, compared to the great multitude profeffing Chriftianity, but all defcended from the former Jews in the land of Ifrael, the forefathers of the prefent vifible ones; which were, at different times, led captives into all nations: your lives are long, their's but fhort; your are the holy feed, the people and faints of the Moft High; to whom, and your children for ever, belongs the poffeffion and government of his kingdom.

The Lord God, who was the Lord Jefus Chrift, commands me now, and not until now, to infert the following teftimonies, *as a warning to all blafphemers*, and as a reafon to all men, that do not know, why he faid to me, in the preceding part of this book, You may inform the king of England that I call you my nephew.

THE GOSPEL ST. MATTHEW.

CHAP. XII.

46 While he (meaning Chrift) yet talked to the people, behold his mother and his brethren ftood without, defiring to speak with him.

CHAP. XIII.

36 Then Jesus sent the multitude away, and went into the house; and his disciples came to him, saying, Declare to us the parable of the tares of the field.

37 He answered, and said to them, He that soweth the good seed is the son of man.

38 The field is the world; the good seed are the children of the kingdom; but the tares are the children of the wicked one; the enemy that sowed them is the devil; the harvest is the end of the world; and the reapers are the angels.

40 As therefore the tares are gathered and burned in the fire, so shall it be also in the end of this world.

41. The son of man shall send forth his angels, and they shall gather out of his kingdom all things that offend, and them which do iniquity, and shall cast them into a furnace of fire, there shall be wailing and gnashing of teeth.

43 Then shall the righteous shine forth as the sun in the kingdom of their father. Who hath ears to hear, let him hear.

47 Again, the kingdom of heaven is like to a net that was cast into the sea, and gathered of every kind; which, when it was full, they drew to shore, and sat down, and gathered the good into vessels, but cast the bad away.

49 So shall it be at the end of the world: the angels shall come forth, and sever the wicked from among the just. And shall cast them down into the furnace of fire; there shall be wailing and gnashing of teeth.

51 Jesus says to them, Have ye understood all these things? They say to him, Yea, Lord.

53 And it came to pass, that when Jesus had finished these parables, he departed thence. And when he was come into his own country, he taught them in their synagogue; insomuch that they were astonished, and said, Whence has this man this wisdom, and these mighty works?

55 Is not this the carpenter's son? Is not his mother called Mary? And his brethren (meaning his brothers) James, and Joses, and Simon, and Judas?

56 And his sisters, are they not all with us? Whence then has this man all these things? And they were offended at him. But Jesus said to them, A prophet is not without honour, save in his own country, and in his own house.

After the Lord Jesus Christ was born of the blessed Virgin Mary, she was married to Joseph; by whom she had sons and daughters: they were supposed, as the unquestionable testimony of the Gospel demonstrates, to be his brothers and sisters.

St. Paul, the apostle, and likewise St. Mark, has left on record similar testimonies, which corroborate the preceding one.

Being, myself, descended from that James, *the eldest son of Mary, by Joseph,* whom St. Paul calls the Lord's brother, is the reason that the Lord God, who was the

Lord Jesus Christ, said to me, as an expression of fondness, and to manifest his regard, *You may* inform the king of England that I call you my nephew.

ST. PAUL, GALATIANS,

CHAP. I.

19 But other of the apostles saw I none, save James, the Lord's brother.

ST. MARK,

CHAP VI.

2 And when the sabbath day was come, He (meaning Christ) began to teach in the synagogue; and many hearing him were astonished, saying, From whence has this man these things? and what wisdom is this which is given to him, that even such mighty works are wrought by his hands?

3 Is not this the carpenter, the son of Mary, the brother of James and Joses, and of Juda and Simon? And are not his sisters here with us? And they were offended at him.

The Lord God commands me to say, for the information and warning of all men, That between this day the 25th of the present month called October, and the beginning of the month called June 1795, without mentioning to any person at what particular time in that interval, my revelation to the Jews, with a sign the same as Moses in Egypt—and to the people of London, will take place : *to the former*, to receive the commands of God through me and to collect all their property and depart in great haste from all nations to their own land : the ships of England, France, Spain, and all Europe, will be obedient to the commands of God to carry home their wealth, and all the people that chuse to go by sea; *to the latter*, to convince them the destruction of London in 1791, according to the eighteenth chapter of the Revelation, would have been fulfilled, but for my entreaty. To fulfil *the 4th chapter and the 5th verse of the* prophet *Malachi*, which is, Behold, I will send you Elijah the prophet before the coming of the great and dreadful day of the Lord. I myself, am the appointed prophet to fulfil that chapter and character. Therefore I warn all people in all nations —that the terrible day of the Lord, alluded to, is nigh; it is not the day of univerſal judgment, but the day which is to burn like an oven, and which is to conſume the wicked from the face of the earth—like the ſtubble of the field. Then, according to the prophet Daniel in the ſeventh chapter, the kingdom, and dominion, and the greatneſs of the kingdom under the whole heaven, will be given for an everlaſting poſſeſſion to the people and ſaints of the Moſt High. Being to be revealed the ſame as Moſes, but in the ſame Spirit and power as Elijah, when he deſtroyed the ſoldiers and prieſts of Ahab, I am to re-pronounce his judgments, to execute them on all falſe Chriſts and falſe prophets; and afterwards, to call down fire from heaven to conſume the enemies of God.

The Lord God commands me to ſay to you, *William Bryan*, that you are of the the Hebrews, and of the tribe of Judah; and that you, with *John Wright*, are appointed, and will be commanded by him, to teſtify pub-licly to the world who I now am, and what my future deſignation is.

The Lord God will influence and command numbers of his people, both men and women, to give the ſame publick teſtimonies. He will alſo give them, to fulfil the *prophecy of Joel in the 2d chapter*, in wonderful viſions, dreams, and open ſigns in the heaven, a knowledge of the approaching times.

28 And it ſhall come to paſs afterward that I will pour out my Spirit upon all fleſh; and your ſons and your daughters ſhall prophecy; your old men ſhall dream dreams, and your young men ſhall ſee viſions.

29 And alſo upon the ſervants and upon the hand-maids in thoſe days, I will pour out my Spirit.

30 And I will ſhew wonders in the heavens and in the earth; blood, and fire, and pillars of ſmoke.

31 The ſun ſhall be turned into darkneſs, and the moon into blood, before the great and terrible day of the Lord come.

32 And it ſhall come to paſs, that whoſoever ſhall call on the name of the Lord ſhall be delivered: for in mount Zion and in Jeruſalem ſhall be deliverance, as the Lord has ſaid, *And in the remnant whom the Lord ſhall call.*

THE REVELATION TO ST. JOHN,

CHAP. VI.

Which relates to the present war—its progress—and consequences; and its destruction by the woeful but just judgment of an offended God.

And I saw when the Lamb opened one of the seals, and I heard as it were the sound of thunder; one of the four beasts saying, Come and see. And I saw, and behold a white horse; and he that sat on him had a bow; and a crown was given to him; and he went forth conquering, and to conquer.

3 And when he had opened the second seal, I heard the second beast say, Come and see. And there went out another horse that was red; and power was given to him that sat thereon to take peace from the earth, and that they should kill one another and there was given to him a great sword.

5 And when he had opened the third seal, I heard the third beast say, Come and see. And I beheld, and lo, a black horse; and he that sat on him had a pair of balances in his hand. And I heard a voice in the midst of the four beasts say, A measure of wheat for a penny, and three measures of barley for a penny, and see thou hurt not the oil and the wine.

7 And when he had opened the fourth seal, I heard the voice of the fourth beast say, Come and see. And I looked, and behold a pale horse; and his name that sat on him was Death, and hell followed with him: and power was given to them over the fourth part of the earth, to kill with sword, and with hunger, and with death, and with the beasts of the earth.

9 And when he had opened the fifth seal, I saw under the altar the souls of them that were slain for the word of God, and for the testimony which they held. And they cried with a loud voice, saying, How long, O Lord, holy and true, dost thou not judge and avenge our blood on them that dwell on the earth. And white robes were given to every one of them; and it was said to them, That they should rest yet for a little season, until their

fellow servants also and their brethren, that should be killed as they were, should be fulfilled.

The fifth seal is now opened, and the secret prophecy contained under it is published for the information and benefit of all men.

The opening of the next seal, while it brings woe to the wicked, will manifest to the Jews the great power and name of their prince with God, as recorded by Daniel, for their deliverance and restoration.

THE PROPHET DANIEL,

CHAP. XII.

And at that time shall Michael stand up, the great prince which stands for the children of thy people; and there shall be a time of trouble, such as never was since there was a nation, even to that same time; *and at that time thy people shall be delivered*, every one that shall be found written in the book.

The time of the world alluded to, when the woeful calamities mentioned here will take place, is just now come: Myself, who will be the revealed prince of Israel, is the Michael and the great prince alluded to here by the angel speaking to Daniel: but not the Lord Jesus Christ visibly, who is God, and King over all: neither is it the angel that is mentioned under the name of Michael *in the 10th chapter and 13th verse.*

2 And many of them that sleep in the dust of the earth shall awake; some to everlasting life, and some to shame and everlasting contempt.

3 And they that be wise shall shine as the brightness of the firmament; and they that turn many to righteousness, as the stars for ever and ever.

4 But thou, O Daniel, shut up the words, and seal the book, *even to the time of the end:* many shall run to and fro, and knowledge shall be increased.

8 And I heard, but understood not: then said I, O, my Lord, what shall be the end of these things?

9 And he said, Go thy way, Daniel; for the words are closed up and sealed *till the time of the end.*

10 Many shall be purified, and made white, and tried;

but the wicked shall do wickedly; and none of the wicked shall understand; but the wise shall understand.

At this time, which is the time alluded to by the angel informing Daniel, the earth will quake, and be rent in many places: the heaven will be convulsed, opening and shutting, and shewing many fearful signs: there will be storms of wind, hail, and showers of rain, with violent thundering and lightning: the very beasts of the field, birds of the air, and fishes of the sea, will be frightened: all the inhabitants of the earth will tremble for their lives, dreading that it is the hour of their diffolution and day of univerfal judgment; so fierce and terrible will the great anger of God be manifested against a wicked world, profeffing Chrift with their lips, but teaching rebellion against his bleffed Gofpel in their public laws and forms of prayer.

Swearing oaths; the Lord's Supper, or taking the facrament to remember him and commemorate the awful moment when he gave it to his difciples, is made a qualification, even to the moft unthinking, abandoned, and wicked, to ferve in any public office or employment whatever.

Of the public prayers. Our Father, which art in heaven; hallowed be thy name; thy kingdom come; *which is the kingdom of peace*; is very good: but the next form of prayer is befeeching God to go forth with fleets and armies: this is very bad, becaufe it is in direct oppofition to the former; it encourages ftrife, hatred, war, and bloodfhed; it is calling on God to keep back his kingdom, and to overthrow his own Gofpel of peace. The worfhip of Chriftians ought to be pure, humble, and peaceable, without any mixture of politics or directional conftraints from human law.

The bifhops are called Lords Spiritual. To ordain a clergyman, he muft kneel down before a bifhop, while he fays, "Receive the Holy Ghoft for the office and work of a prieft in the church of God, now committed unto thee by the impofition of our hands. Whofe fins thou doft forgive, they are forgiven; and whofe fins thou doft retain, they are retained."

Likewife, at the confecration of a bifhop, it is faid,

" Receive the Holy Ghost for the office and work of a bishop in the church of God, now committed unto thee by the imposition of our hands; in the name of the Father, and of the Son, and of the Holy Ghost. Amen. And remember that thou stir up the grace of God, which is given thee *by this imposition of our hands.*"

As there is in truth no Lord but God, no man ought to assume his sacred name. No man is Spiritual that has not the Holy Ghost, the divine Spirit of truth; it is by Christ that it is given, and he will not give it to any that promotes the evil of war and disobedience to his Gospel. A prince may give to a man a title, but it is God only that can make him Spiritual; he cannot give that mighty Spirit which he has not the power to command, and which he never received the gift of himself. To pursue then any longer such a false form of ordination and consecration, is not only dishonourable to the king, parliament, and people of England, but also a reproach to the bishops to attempt to give, and to the clergy to kneel down to receive.

Turn from such deceitful unmanly ways, and endeavour to live long; for it is the word of God through a man that points at the crime, and warns you to forsake what must, if you do not, lead to certain death! for, believe me, the day of destruction to punish disobedience to the Gospel is so very nigh, that it will take place before the commencement of eight months from this day.

Look at your wives, your children, and all that is dear to you on earth; then consider how great the blessing to have them, to live with and possess them; but how terrible the evil to separate, to be burnt with fire— to die, and lose them for ever!

Remember, God created man in his own image and likeness, and created the earth for his use; that man might believe in him and obey his commands.

He brought the children of Israel out of Egypt to conduct them to the promised land; but when they disobeyed him in the wilderness, he destroyed thousands of them. He burnt Sodom and Gomorrah, because the people were wicked; but he saved Nineveh, which was also denounced, because the people repented.

The Lord God is great, merciful, and compassionate

to forgive all that do entreat, and obey his commands; but be assured, he is also great, mighty, and powful, jealous of his sacred name and honour: when given to men; and he can do now what he did of old, *they are recorded for our example and warning*; that is, overthrow cities, and destroy multitudes in an instant.

Life, blessing, and peace, is the inheritance of the servants, the saints, and people of the Most High.

REVELATION.

CHAP. VI. CONTINUED.

12. And I beheld when he had opened the sixth seal, and lo, there was a great earthquake; and the sun became black as sackcloth of hair, and the moon became as blood; and the stars of heaven fell to the earth, even as a fig tree casts her untimely figs when she is shaken by a mighty wind; and the heaven departed as a scroll when it is rolled together; and every mountain and island were moved out of their places.

15. And the kings of the earth, and the great men, and the rich men, and the chief captains, and the mighty men, and every bondsman, and every free man, hid themselves in the dens, and in the rocks of the mountains; and said to the mountains and rocks, Fall on us, and hide us from the face of him that sits on the throne, and from the wrath of the Lamb; for the great day of his wrath is come; and who shall be able to stand?

SECOND BOOK OF ESDRAS.

CAAP. II.

42. I, Esdrass, saw upon the mount Zion a great multitude of people, whom I could not number, and they all praised the Lord with songs.

43. And in the midst of them there was a young man of a high stature, taller than all the rest, and upon every one of their heads he set crowns, and was more exalted; which I marvelled at greatly.

44. So I asked the angel, and said, Sir, what are these? He answered and said to me, These be they that have put off the mortal cloathing, and put on the immortal: (It means the Jews, who, when I am revealed, will acknow-

ledge that the Lord Chrift is the Lord God; then they will put off the mortal cloathing of unbelief and error, and put on the immortal cloathing of faith and righteoufnefs,) and have confeffed the name of God: now are they crowned, and receive palms.

46 Then faid I to the angel, What young perfon is that which crowns them, and gives them palms in their hands. So he anfwered and faid to me, It is the Son of God, whom they have confeffed in the world. Then I began greatly to commend them that ftood fo ftiffly for the name of the Lord.

The Son of God, alluded to here, is not the Saviour, the Lord Jefus Chrift, as has been always erroneoufly fuppofed; but a human being, of flefh and blood, like any other. It is a man, and but a man; though recorded, and honoured with being called the Son of God. It is myfelf, who am the man that will be made that prince, alluded to by Ezekiel, in the xliv. xlv. xlvi. and xlviii. chapters of his Prophecy; and in the fecond chapter of Haggai, *when kingdoms are convulfed with violence and war, with the fall of thrones and the deftruction of armies,* as a promifed, a defigned fignet, manifefted to the world by the great power and extended goodnefs of God. It is that man, whom God has defigned to be the vifible prince of Ifrael. As a believer in God, *by, and through Chrift, the divine Spirit of Truth,* and an obeyer of his commands, he is a fon, an adopted fon: fo is every man under heaven an acknowledged fon, whether rich or poor, that does the fame; and fo is every woman likewife, an adopted, an acknowledged daughter.

Remember the words of the Lord Jefus Chrift in the Gofpel, where he fays, After this manner therefore pray ye. Our Father, which art in heaven, &c. As God then is our father, we, that acknowledge and pray to him as fuch, are furely his fons and daughters.

All that believe in the teftimony of God by me, which he now commands me to make known, are his people, a part *(becaufe the vifible Jews are the great body)* of that innumerable multitude, fhewn by the angel to Efdras, crowned, and receiving palms.

The Lord God commands me to remind all people of the loud thunder that was on the 7th of Auguft laft, and

K

to fay, It was a threat from him to deftroy London, fooner than fuffer me to be hurt: take it for a warning, and beware of the dreadful confequences that will moft certainly enfue, if a fimilar injury is intended againft me: for if you, the Englifh Government, are determined to moleft me, the Lord God is alfo determined to oppofe you; and will vifit with death on his enemies, and with deftruction on their capital. For the Englifh Government, *both what is called civil and ecclefiftical*, in its prefent form, will, by the fierce anger and determined judgment of the Lord God, be removed, annihilated, and utterly deftroyed, before the expiration of ten months from this day.

For thofe unhappy men, which compofe it, as if the injuftice of the prefent war was not fufficient to provoke him, have imprudently gone on, adding evil to evil, and now, more than before, publicly encourage blafphemy againft him, and abufe againft his prophet. Why do they do fo? faid the Lord God to me. Why? becaufe you have not their *mark*, but my feal; you have not their authority, the laying on the hands of their bifhops, to give the Holy Ghoft to prophecy by, but my Spirit, *yet thefe are not the men that pretend to judge of fpirits*, to difcern the good from the evil: they fuppofe every man, that writes or fpeaks under the power and influence of God, is a falfe prophet, an impofter under delufion; becaufe the words of truth, by him, go to contradict their mark, their human ordinances, and political forms of prayer.

The Lord Jefus Chrift fays, in the fifteenth chapter of his Gofpel by St. Matthew, " But in vain they do worfhip me, teaching, for doctrines, the commandments of men.

And becaufe the annunciation of my kingdom of peace and prefervation, brings with it the fentence of death againft their kingdom of war and human deftruction; therefore, hear what the Lord God fays to me by revelation, and commands me to write, That, as they have encouraged blafphemy againft me, they fhall not profper; for I will fend a blaft on them that will confound all their counfels: and, as they have encouraged abufe againft you, whom I fent, and who entreated me for their good, I will deliver them over to the power of their enemies; to be hated by every body, despised, and trod under foot like mire in the streets.

The Lord God commands me to say, for the information of the English government, the judges, and all men, that the prisoners, now in confinement, and on trial for their lives, charged with the crime of High Treason against the life of the king of England, are innocent, as such, he requires me to make known to the king his sacred commands in writing, and to publish this for the knowledge of all.

The Lord God commands me to inform, through this book, all that honour him—his servants—the peaceable and righteous in all nations, which have had their property, whether in land or money, confiscated, for no other reason than because the nation they belonged to declared war against the nation they lived in, all such property, or its full value, with reasonable interest for the time, shall most surely be restored.

And you, Peter Woulfe, one of the Avignon Society, whom the Lord my God commands me to mention here by name, as a testimony of his great regard, your property, confiscated in France, will all be restored with interest, and much kindness shewn to you by the members of its government: they will restore the property of every other *peaceable individual* likewise: by the same divine rule of justice, Spain, England, Prussia, Germany, Holland, and all the other nations of Europe, must restore theirs. For the time of the world is just now come, and God is firmly determined to manifest his mighty power, for the preservation of his people and saints, by fulfilling by me his words in the eleventh chapter of Isaiah, a part of which are—But with righteousness he will judge the poor, and reprove, with equity, for the meek of the earth; and he shall smite the earth with the rod of his mouth, and with the breath of his lips he shall slay the wicked.

RICHARD BROTHERS.

London, No. 57, Paddington Street,
  26th of the month called October, 1794.

THE PROPHET ISAIAH,

CHAP. XLI.

25 I HAVE raised up one from the north, (meaning the revealed Prince of the Hebrews at this time,) and he shall come; (meaning to Jerusalem, from that northern part of the world alluded to: England lies in the north, and it is indeed the country meant:) from the rising of the sun he shall call upon my name: and he shall come upon princes as upon mortar, and as the potter treads clay.

Isaiah stood at Jerusalem when this prophecy was given, writing and recording it by the direction of God, he looked to the northern part of the world, where this distinguished person, which he so clearly mentions, is first to rise, and then come to Jerusalem, calling on the name of the Lord, from the rising to the setting of the sun; as zealous for an obedience to the Gospel, as David, his father, was for the law: travelling in the mighty strength of the Spirit, and armed with the divine power of fire, like Elijah, * he will subject nations, remove thrones, and burn all rebel princes.

26 Who hath declared from the beginning, that we may know; and before the time, (meaning before the prophecy is fulfilled; it being 2461 years from its declaration then to its accomplishment, now this present year of 1795,) that we may say, He is righteous! yea, there is none that sheweth; yea, there is none that declareth; yea, there is none that heareth your words.

The king of England, and the members of his government, the parliament, bishops, judges, and all the ambassadors from foreign nations, in Londen, have received the information of their fall and destruction; but they all refuse to believe, and by so doing fulfil exactly what the prophet means, when he says Yea, there is none that heareth your words.

27 The first shall say to Zion, Behold, behold them;

---

* Malachi. iv. 1 and 5. Isaiah, xi. 4. II. Esdras, xiii. 11.

(meaning the Jews crowding home to Jerufalem in great multitudes,) and I will give to Jerufalem one that bringeth good tidings. (It means the revealed prince, returning home with the people, to rebuild the defolate city, and make her rejoice.)

28 For I beheld, and there was no man; even among them there was no counfellor that, when I afked of them, could anfwer a word.

Here the Holy Ghoft, the fpirit of God, fpoke by Ifaiah, as if fpeaking by myfelf at this very hour; for I have fent books of the judgments of God to the king of England, and the members of his government, his parliament, his bifhops, his judges, and all the foreign ambaffadors in London, for their refpective countries: but to accomplifh what is fo faithfully recorded by the prophet, where he fpeaks fpiritually as myfelf—Even among them there was no counfellor that, when I fent to them, could anfwer a word.

29 Behold, they are all vanity; their works are nothing; their molten images are wind and confufion.

Other Parts of the Revelation to St. John which are to be fulfilled, and which the Lord God commands me now to publifh.

CHAP. XIII.

1 And I ftood upon the fand of the fea, and faw a beaft rife up out of the fea, having feven heads and ten horns; and upon his horns ten crowns, and upon his heads the name of Blafphemy.

This beaft means the Englifh Monarchy; and it is by fhips and commerce that it has rofe from the fea to fuch aftonifhing grandeur and magnitude. The heads, horns, and crowns, allude to the many departments of Government, and their fplendid diftinctions. The Blafphemy means the titles given to, and affumed by the King of England; fuch as, Our Moft Gracious Sovereign Lord, Sacred Perfon, Majefty, Defender of the Faith, and Supreme Head of the Church; all which names belong to

God, he only can be what they exprefs, and when they applied to any other, the fin is Blafphemy in his fight.

2 And the beaft which I faw was like unto a leopard, and his feet were as the feet of a bear, and his mouth as the mouth of a lion; and the dragon gave him his power, and his feat, and great authority.

The Englifh Monarchy, for being Supreme Head of the Church, and over the many religious fects tolerated in the country, is the reafon that it is, for their great number, compared to a leopard full of fpots.

As a bear is very ftrong on his feet, fo is the Englifh Monarchy: and as a lion roars with his mouth the loudeft of any beaft, fo does the Englifh Monarchy proclaim its greatnefs more than any other.

3 And I faw one of his heads as it were wounded to death; and his deadly wound was healed: and all the world wondered after the beaft.

The beginning of this verfe means the death of Charles the Firft, king of England: and the deadly wound being healed, means the recovery of the Monarchy by the reftoration of Charles the Second. During the interval of time between the death and fucceffion, all the world wondered if the Englifh Monarchy would ever be reftored again.

9 If any man have an ear let him hear. He that leads into captivity, fhall go into captivity: he that kills with the fword muft be killed with the fword. Here is the patience and the faith of the faints.

The leading into captivity means imprifonment and flavery; and killing with the fword, means violence and war. The patience of the faints is, to bear quietly with thofe evils, and to refift the temptations of wealth to do them: All that have faith in God will not do fuch things, from a belief that they are offenfive, becaufe he commands them not.

11 And I beheld another beaft coming up out of the earth; and he had two horns like a lamb, and he fpake as a dragon.

This verfe means the Elector of Hanover. Coming up out of the earth, is to fignify that his country or government is fituated inland. The horns of a lamb, and the voice of a dragon, means, that although he is weak in power like a lamb, yet by his voice he can threaten in great and mighty words like a dragon.

12 And he exerciseth all the power of the first beast before him, &c.

It means the Elector of Hanover's succession to the crown, place, and power of the former King of England. To fulfil this part of the prophecy given by Revelation to St. John, the utter expulsion of the Stuart family must against all human opposition have taken place to admit the Elector of Hanover.

A great part of this chapter is taken up in describing the king and parliament. I am commanded to inform both of the recorded judgments of God, the dangers which threaten them, and their certainty of taking place, unless they implore him for mercy, and obtain it.

They have individually promised, by their godfathers and godmothers, in the sacred covenant of baptism, and acknowledge a confirmation of it by receiving the sacrament (for both were instituted by the Lord Jesus Christ) to believe in him and obey his commands: yet, notwithstanding this heaviest of all obligations which a human being can enter into (for it is with his God) and on the performance of which his salvation depends, the laws they make, a part of the Thirty-nine Articles, and some of the forms of prayer, used in public worship, goes more to break the covenant of baptism, to dishonour God, and oppose an obedience to his blessed Gospel, than was ever authorised in any other nation.

Without submitting to the forms of law prescribed by act of parliament, which are in direct opposition to the commands of Christ, and very sinful to do, no man can hold any place or profit of trust, enjoy the privilege of freedom, and comparatively to buy or sell.

17 And that no man might buy or sell, save he that had the mark, or the name of the beast, or the number of his name.

18 Here is wisdom. Let him that hath understanding count the number of the beast; for it is the number of a man; and his number is six hundred threescore and six.

This verse means the English parliament; and although it exceeds the number mentioned here, yet, notwithstanding, it is the real and very assembly of men alluded to in the Revelation, by the number of 666.

Because the Parliament acknowledge and address the king by the divine names which belong only to God; such as, Our Most Gracious Sovereign Lord, Sire, Majesty, and honour him with equal humility in supplication, when they require any thing, as if he really was the Lord of heaven and earth; such as, Humbly praying that your Majesty would be most graciously pleased, &c. Therefore God, in his great anger, being jealous of his name and honour, calls the king a beast, and the parliament his image and number.

CHAP. XIV.

1 And I looked, and lo, a lamb stood on the mount Sion, and with him a hundred and forty-four thousand, having his father's name written in their foreheads.

The lamb, mentioned here, means myself as Prince of the Hebrews; and mount Sion, Jerusalem: The hundred and forty-four thousand with me, having the name of my father wrote in their foreheads, means not only the visible Jews of the twelve tribes, but likewise the invisible:—it comprehends all of the Hebrew extraction that will believe in the testimony of God by me.

6 And I saw another angel fly in the midst of heaven, having the everlasting Gospel, to preach to them that dwell on the earth, and to every nation, and kindred, and tongue, and people; saying, with a loud voice, Fear God, and give glory to him, for the hour of his judgment is come. and worship him that made heaven and earth, and the sea, and the fountains of waters.

8 And there followed another angel, saying, Babylon is fallen, is fallen; that great city! because she made all nations drink of the wine of the wrath of her fornication.

9 And the third angel followed them, saying, with a loud voice, If any man worship the beast, and his image, and receive his mark in his forehead, or in his hand, the same shall drink of the wine of the wrath of God, which is poured out without mixture into the cup of his indig-

nation; and he shall be tormented with fire and brimstone, in the presence of the holy angels, and in the presence of the lamb: and the smoke of their torment ascends up for ever and ever; and they have no rest day nor night, who worship the beast and his image, and whosoever receives the mark of his name.

12 Here is the patience of the saints: here are they that keep the commandments of God, and the faith of Jesus.

CHAP. XVI.

1 And I heard a great voice out of the temple, saying to the seven angels, Go your ways, and pour out the vials of the wrath of God upon the earth.

2 And the first went, and poured out his vial upon the earth; and there fell a noisome and grievous sore on the men which had the mark of the beast, and on them which worshipped his image. And the second angel poured out his vial upon the sea, and it became as the blood of a dead man; and every living soul died in the sea.

4 And the third angel poured out his vial upon the rivers and fountains of waters; and they became blood. And I heard the angel of the waters say, Thou art righteous, O Lord, which art, and was, and shalt be; because thou hast judged thus. For they have shed the blood of saints and prophets, and thou hast given them blood to drink; for they are worthy.

10 And the fifth angel poured out his vial upon the seat of the beast, and his kingdom was full of darkness, and they gnawed their tongues for pain; and blasphemed the God of heaven, because of their pains and their sores, and repented not of their deeds.

CHAP. XXI.

6 And he said to me, It is done, I am Alpha and Omega, the beginning and the end: I will give to him that is a-thirst of the fountain of the water of life freely. He that overcometh shall inherit all things; and I will be his God, and he shall be my son.

8 But the fearful and unbelieving, and the abominable and murderers, and whoremongers, and forcerers, and idolaters, and all liars, shall have their part in the lake which burns with fire and brimstone; which is the second death.

The Lord God commands me to say to you, George the Third, king of England, that immediately on my being revealed, in London, to the Hebrews as their Prince, and to all nations as their Governor, your crown must be delivered up to me, that all your power and authority may instantly cease. On my being revealed, the invisible power of the angel of God, which guards me now, will then become visible as a flame of fire; the very same that accompanied Moses and the children of Israel out of Egypt. I must not acknowledge any superior but the Lord Christ, who is the Lord God: and as a man raised up, like David, by him to be a Prince, he commands me to allow no equal, but instantly to burn out of his kingdom the rebellious and disobedient. Read the xli. chap. and verse 25, of Isaiah.

Be advised by this, for evil is going to be let loose; when it is, the king of England will no more believe the signs of God by me than the King of Egypt would by Moses; therefore, desire your servants to deliver directly to you all letters and messages from me; for, it is for your contempt to me that your country is ordered to be invaded, and your power to be destroyed. The tall oak, with all its branches cut off, mentioned in one of the visions of God, in the preceding part of this book, means yourself and family.

The Lord God commands me to say to you, Nathaniel Brassey Halhed, that as you are reviled and considered, by your former acquaintances, as ruined and lost, for speaking the truth as he manifested it to you, for publishing your testimony of me, his servant, you shall, by the expiration of three months, from this day, have your choice of being either Governor General of India, or President of the Board of Controul in England; that all men may be convinced, that he that rules in heaven is able to exalt or to abase; that he is still able, even at this late hour of a wicked world, to reward the obedient to his blessed Spirit, and give the most eminent places on earth to whomsoever he pleases.

The Lord God commands me to inform all men, as a prevention, in future, to their asking unnecessary questions, that all that is proper and allowable for me to relate, from him, is published in this book.

The Copy of a LETTER *to* WILLIAM PITT, *Chancellor of the Exchequer, which the Lord God commands me now to publish.*

IN obedience to the sacred command of the Lord God, whose servant and prophet I am, I inform the chancellor of the Exchequer, that the prisoners now in confinement, and on trial, charged with the crime of High Treason against the King's Life, are innocent.

I am likewise commanded to inform you, because God is very merciful and compassionate, that the seventh chapter of the prophecy of Daniel, and last part of the sixth chapter in the Revelation to St. John, will be fulfilled before the expiration of seven months from this day. And also my revelation to the Hebrews, as their Prince and Leader, according to the twelfth chapter of the prophecy of Daniel; to the king and people of England, and the people of all nations, as their Ruler—for—and immediately under God, according to the twenty-second chapter of the Second Book of Samuel; to all nations, as the promised *Signet of Peace,* according to the second chapter of Haggai; and as Elijah, to the wicked, the revilers, and blasphemers against God, according to the fourth chapter of Malachi.

RICHARD BROTHERS.

No. 57, Paddington Street,
9th of the month called November.

The King, and duke of Portland, as secretary of state, were wrote to at the same time.

REVELATION,

CHAP. XI.

15 And the seventh angel sounded, and there were great voices in heaven, saying, The kingdoms of this world are become the kingdoms of our Lord, and of his Christ; and he shall reign for ever and ever.

RICHARD BROTHERS,

The man that will be revealed to the Hebrews as their Prince; to all nations as their Governor; according to the covenant to King David, immediately under God.

London, No. 57, Paddington Street,
20th of the month called February, 1795.

www.ingramcontent.com/pod-product-compliance
Lightning Source LLC
Chambersburg PA
CBHW022135160426
43197CB00009B/1300